101 Skills

Kids Need

To Learn

How to Cook, Clean,

Learn about Money and Mindset and

Everything Else

Benny White

Book Cover by Benny White

Illustrations by Benny White

1st edition 2023

Table of Contents

Introduction

As children grow and develop, it's important for them to learn a range of skills that will help them succeed in life. From understanding themselves and managing their emotions to operating appliances and embracing challenges, life skills are essential tools that children can use to navigate the world around them.

In this book, "Life Skills for Kids," we explore a range of topics designed to help kids build the skills they need to thrive. From learning effective skills and understanding self-control, to reflecting on failure and embracing challenges, this book provides practical advice and real-life examples that kids can use to develop their life skills.

Whether you're a parent, teacher, or caregiver, "Life Skills for Kids" is the perfect guide to help young people develop the skills they need to succeed. So join us on this journey as we explore the important life skills that will help kids grow into confident and capable adults.

Recognizing Yourself

In order to be successful in life, it's important to have a good understanding of who you are and what makes you unique. In this chapter, we'll explore some of the key concepts of self-awareness and self-discovery that can help you develop a better understanding of yourself.

One of the first steps in understanding yourself is to understand your emotions. Emotions are a normal part of life and help us understand how we're feeling at any given moment. However, it's important to be able to identify and manage your emotions, so that they don't control you.

Some tips for understanding and managing your emotions include:

Recognizing and labeling your emotions: Try to identify what you're feeling and give it a name. This can help you understand why you're feeling a certain way.

Practicing self-care: Taking care of yourself, such as getting enough sleep, exercise, and eating well, can help you manage your emotions more effectively.

Expressing your feelings in a healthy way: Find healthy ways to express your emotions, such as talking to a trusted friend or family member, writing in a journal, or participating in a creative activity.

Another important aspect of understanding yourself is to identify your strengths and weaknesses. By understanding what you're good at and what you need to work on, you can focus on developing your skills and becoming the best version of yourself.

Some tips for identifying your strengths and weaknesses include:

Asking for feedback: Seek feedback from others to get a better understanding of your strengths and weaknesses.

Reflecting on your experiences: Think about times when you felt confident and successful, and also times when you struggled. This can help you identify your strengths and areas for improvement.

Trying new things: Don't be afraid to step outside your comfort zone and try new things. This can help you discover new talents and interests.

In conclusion, understanding yourself is an important step in developing your life skills. By understanding your emotions, strengths, and weaknesses, you can become more self-aware and better equipped to navigate the challenges of life.

Monitoring Yourself

Self-monitoring or self-control is the ability to regulate your thoughts, feelings and behaviors in order to achieve your goals. It's an important life skill that can help you navigate difficult situations and make better decisions. In this subchapter, we'll explore some of the key concepts of self-control and provide tips for developing this important skill.

<u>Understanding Impulsivity</u>

Impulsivity is the tendency to act on a whim without considering the consequences of your actions. While a certain degree of impulsiveness can be normal and even fun, excessive impulsivity can lead to problems in many areas of life, such as relationships, work, and finances.

Tips for Developing Self-Control

Practice mindfulness: Mindfulness is the practice of being present in the moment and focusing on your thoughts and feelings without judgment. By practicing mindfulness, you can gain a better understanding of your thoughts and emotions and develop better self-control.

Set achievable goals: Setting achievable goals can help you stay focused and motivated, and also provide a sense of accomplishment when you reach your goals.

Practice delay of gratification: Delaying gratification means waiting to satisfy a desire or need until a later time. By practicing this skill, you can learn to control your impulses and make better decisions.

Surround yourself with positive role models: Surrounding yourself with positive role models who exhibit self-control can help you develop this important skill.
Develop a growth mindset: A growth mindset is the belief that you can learn and grow through challenges and failures. By developing a growth mindset, you can learn to view setbacks as opportunities for growth and development.

Self-control is a critical life skill that can help you make better decisions, achieve your goals, and lead a fulfilling life. By practicing mindfulness, setting achievable goals, delaying gratification, surrounding yourself with positive role models, and developing a growth mindset, you can develop this important skill and become more self-aware and capable.

Other Ways to Improve Self-Control

Get enough sleep: Lack of sleep can impair self-control, so it's important to get enough sleep to help you make better decisions.

Exercise regularly: Exercise has been shown to improve self-control, so it's important to make time for physical activity in your daily routine.

Manage stress: Chronic stress can impair self-control, so it's important to manage stress through techniques such as deep breathing, meditation, and relaxation.
Avoid tempting situations: By avoiding tempting situations, you can reduce the likelihood of giving into impulsiveness and make better decisions.

Practice self-reflection: Regular self-reflection can help you understand your thoughts and emotions and develop better self-control.

<u>Using Self-Control in Real Life Situations</u>

Self-control can be particularly challenging in real-life situations, such as when you're faced with temptation, stress, or frustration. Here are some tips for using self-control in real-life situations:

Take a deep breath: Taking a deep breath can help you calm down and regulate your emotions.

Count to 10: Counting to 10 can give you time to calm down and make a better decision.

Identify your triggers: Understanding your triggers can help you avoid tempting situations and reduce the likelihood of impulsiveness.

Seek support: Talking to someone you trust can help you regulate your emotions and make better decisions.

In conclusion, self-control is a critical life skill that can help you navigate difficult situations and make better decisions. By practicing mindfulness, setting achievable goals, delaying gratification, surrounding yourself with positive role models, and developing a growth mindset, you can improve self-control and lead a more fulfilling life. Additionally, getting enough sleep, exercising regularly, managing stress, avoiding tempting situations, and practicing self-reflection can help you develop this important skill and become more self-aware and capable.

Developing Actual Skills

Learning new skills is essential for personal growth and development. Whether it's learning a new language, playing a musical instrument, or developing a new hobby, learning new skills can help you achieve your goals and improve your well-being.

Learning new skills has numerous benefits, including:

Improving self-esteem and confidence: When you learn a new skill, you build confidence and self-esteem by accomplishing something new and challenging.

Enhancing cognitive function: Learning new skills keeps your brain active and helps to improve cognitive function, such as memory and attention.
Fostering creativity: Learning new skills can help you develop your creativity and find new ways to express yourself.

Building new relationships: Learning a new skill can help you connect with others who share similar interests, and can lead to new friendships and professional connections.

Here are some steps you can follow to effectively learn a new skill:

Identify a skill you want to learn: Choose a skill that interests you and aligns with your goals.

Set achievable goals: Decide what you want to achieve and set achievable goals for yourself.

Find a mentor or teacher: Seek out someone who has experience and knowledge in the skill you want to learn.

Practice consistently: Regular practice is essential for learning a new skill. Set aside dedicated time each day to practice.

Seek feedback: Seek feedback from your mentor or teacher to track your progress and make improvements.

Celebrate your progress: Celebrate your progress along the way, and take time to reflect on what you've learned.

Let's say you want to learn how to cook. This is a valuable life skill that can help you become more self-sufficient and enjoy healthier meals. Here's how you could go about learning this new skill:

Identify the skill: Decide that you want to learn how to cook.

Set achievable goals: Start by setting a goal to learn how to cook a few basic dishes, such as scrambled eggs, grilled cheese, and pasta.

Find a mentor or teacher: Ask a parent, grandparent, or family friend who is a good cook to teach you the basics. Or, sign up for a cooking class at a local community center.

Practice consistently: Set aside time each week to practice cooking, and try making one new dish each week.
Seek feedback: Ask for feedback from your mentor or teacher on your cooking skills and how you can improve.

Celebrate your progress: Celebrate your successes, such as cooking a dish that turned out well, or mastering a new technique.

By following these steps, you can effectively learn how to cook and build this new skill into your daily routine. Cooking can also be a fun and rewarding experience, and can lead to a healthier lifestyle and new opportunities to impress others with your culinary creations.

Conclusion

Learning new skills can have a significant impact on your personal and professional growth. By setting achievable goals, finding a mentor or teacher, practicing consistently, seeking feedback, and celebrating your progress, you can effectively learn new skills and achieve your goals. Whether you're looking to improve your well-being, build new relationships, or develop new talents: Learning new skills can help you get there.

Learn from Mistakes

Making mistakes is a natural part of life and a valuable opportunity for growth. In this chapter, we will explore the importance of learning from mistakes and how to turn them into positive experiences.

Mistakes can be frustrating, but they can also provide valuable lessons and insights into our strengths and weaknesses. By embracing mistakes and using them as opportunities to learn and grow, we can become more resilient, confident, and self-aware.

In this chapter, we will discuss strategies for accepting mistakes, taking responsibility for our actions, and using mistakes as opportunities to improve. We will also explore the benefits of reframing failure, seeking feedback, and celebrating our progress.

By learning to embrace mistakes and turn them into opportunities for growth, we can develop the skills and confidence we need to achieve our goals and live a fulfilling life.

Have you ever made a mistake and felt like you wanted to hide under a rock? We all have, but it's important to understand that mistakes are not just inevitable, they are also powerful tools for growth and development. In this chapter, we will delve into the transformative power of mistakes and how we can use them to our advantage.

Think about it, every time we make a mistake, we have a choice. We can either dwell on it, or we can take the experience as an opportunity to learn, grow, and become better. By embracing our mistakes and using them as stepping stones for improvement, we can tap into their unlimited potential and unlock our full potential.

Of course, it's not always easy to look at mistakes in a positive light, but with practice and persistence, we can develop a growth mindset and view challenges and failures as opportunities to learn and grow. This not only helps us overcome adversity, but it also helps us build resilience, confidence, and the courage to tackle new challenges and reach our goals.

So, the next time you make a mistake, don't beat yourself up or hide in shame. Instead, embrace the power of the mistake, learn from it, and use it to become the best version of yourself. Your future self will thank you!

Moreover, when we make a mistake, it can be easy to focus on the negative aspects and let them consume us. However, it's crucial to remember that mistakes are not a reflection of our worth or character, but rather a normal part of the learning process. By shifting our focus from the mistake itself to the lessons we can learn from it, we can gain a new perspective and turn a negative situation into a positive one.

It's important to also understand that making mistakes is a natural part of growth and development. Throughout history, some of the most successful people have attributed their success to the lessons they learned from their mistakes. For example, Thomas Edison failed over 1,000 times before he finally succeeded in inventing the light bulb. Instead of giving up, he embraced his mistakes as opportunities to learn and improve, and his persistence ultimately led to his success.

In conclusion, making mistakes is an inevitable part of life, but it's how we choose to respond to them that determines our success and growth. By embracing mistakes, we can tap into their transformative power and use them to become the best version of ourselves. So, let's embrace the power of mistakes and learn from them!

One real life example of embracing mistakes can be seen in the story of Sarah Blakely, the founder of Spanx. Sarah was working as a door-to-door salesperson for fax machines when she realized there was a need for more comfortable and functional hosiery. She had an idea for footless pantyhose and started working on prototypes in her apartment.

After multiple failed attempts, Sarah was ready to give up on her idea. However, instead of giving up, she embraced her mistakes and used them as opportunities to learn and improve. She took her prototypes to hosiery mills and asked for their feedback. The feedback she received was invaluable and helped her make improvements to her design.

Finally, after many months of hard work and persistence, Sarah launched Spanx, and the rest is history. Today, Spanx is a multi-million dollar company and a household name. Sarah's story is a perfect example of how embracing mistakes can lead to success. By using her mistakes as opportunities to learn and grow, she was able to turn her idea into a thriving business.

Another real life example of embracing mistakes can be seen in the story of Steve Jobs, co-founder of Apple Inc. Steve Jobs was known for his innovative and game-changing ideas, but what many people don't know is that he also made numerous mistakes along the way.

One of the most significant mistakes that Jobs made was his dismissal from Apple in 1985. At the time, Jobs was feeling frustrated with the direction the company was taking and conflicts with the board of directors led to his removal from the company. This could have easily been seen as a defeat, but instead, Jobs used this as an opportunity to learn and grow.

After leaving Apple, Jobs co-founded NeXT, a computer company that focused on high-end computers for the education market. While NeXT was not a huge commercial success, it laid the foundation for Jobs' return to Apple in 1997. Jobs used the lessons he learned at NeXT to help turn around Apple, which was struggling at the time. He introduced new products, such as the iMac, iPod, iPhone, and iPad, which transformed the company and the tech industry as a whole.

In conclusion, Steve Jobs' story is a testament to the power of embracing mistakes. By using his removal from Apple as an opportunity to learn and grow, Jobs was able to not only return to Apple but also lead the company to even greater heights. His story shows us that mistakes are not the end, but rather the beginning of a journey towards growth and success.

It is important to remember that making mistakes is a natural and inevitable part of life. It is through our mistakes that we are able to learn and grow, both as individuals and as a society. However, it is equally important to understand how to handle our mistakes in a constructive manner.

One way to handle mistakes effectively is to adopt a growth mindset. This means approaching challenges and mistakes as opportunities for growth, rather than as insurmountable obstacles. By viewing mistakes as opportunities for growth, we are able to embrace challenges and learn from our mistakes in a positive and productive manner.

Another way to handle mistakes effectively is to take responsibility for our actions. This means acknowledging and accepting the consequences of our mistakes, rather than trying to deflect blame or make excuses. By taking responsibility for our actions, we are able to learn from our mistakes and make positive changes in our lives.

In conclusion, learning from mistakes is a crucial life skill that can help us grow and succeed. By embracing challenges, adopting a growth mindset, and taking responsibility for our actions, we can turn our mistakes into opportunities for growth and success. So the next time you make a mistake, remember that it is not the end, but rather the beginning of a new and exciting journey.

Don't Get Mad

Making mistakes is a normal part of life, and it is important to understand how to handle them in a healthy and productive manner. One of the first steps in handling mistakes is to not get upset. When we make a mistake, it is easy to become overwhelmed by negative emotions such as frustration, anger, or sadness. However, getting upset will not solve the problem or help us learn from the mistake.

So, what can you do instead of getting upset when you make a mistake? One strategy is to take a deep breath and count to ten. This gives you a moment to calm down and collect your thoughts. Another strategy is to think about the mistake objectively, without judgment. Ask yourself questions such as: What happened? What could I have done differently? What can I learn from this? By thinking objectively, you can focus on the facts of the situation, rather than getting caught up in emotions.

It is also helpful to remember that everyone makes mistakes. Even the most successful people in the world have made mistakes. The key is not to dwell on the mistake or beat yourself up over it, but to learn from it and move on.

Finally, it is important to talk to someone about the mistake. This could be a trusted friend, family member, or teacher. Talking about the mistake can help you process your emotions and gain new perspectives on the situation.

In conclusion, when you make a mistake, it is important to not get upset. Instead, take a deep breath, think objectively, remember that everyone makes mistakes, and talk to someone about the situation. By doing these things, you can handle mistakes in a healthy and productive manner, and learn from them in a positive way.

In this subchapter, we have discussed the importance of not getting upset when you make a mistake. This is an essential part of learning from your mistakes and growing as a person. By taking steps to calm down and think objectively about the situation, you can avoid getting bogged down by negative emotions and focus on the opportunities for growth and learning that come with making mistakes.

It is also important to remember that making mistakes is a natural part of life and a crucial part of the learning process. By embracing your mistakes and approaching them with a positive attitude, you can turn challenges into opportunities and develop the resilience and determination you need to succeed in life.

So, the next time you make a mistake, take a deep breath and remember the strategies we have discussed. With time and practice, you will become more and more skilled at handling mistakes in a healthy and productive manner, and you will develop the life skills you need to succeed.

Mistakes Lead To Possibilities

In this subchapter, we will talk about the importance of seeing the opportunity in failure. Failure can be a scary and discouraging experience, but it can also be a powerful opportunity to learn and grow. When you approach failure with a positive attitude and a growth mindset, you can learn important lessons and develop new skills that will help you succeed in the future.

One key strategy for seeing the opportunity in failure is to reflect on what went wrong and what you can do differently next time. This can help you identify areas for improvement and develop a plan for making progress in the future.

Another way to see the opportunity in failure is to look for the silver lining. Even when things don't go as planned, there may still be positives to take away from the situation. For example, you might learn something new about yourself or others, or you might develop a new perspective on the world.

Finally, it is important to remember that failure is a normal part of life and that everyone makes mistakes. By accepting failure as a natural part of the learning process, you can overcome feelings of shame or embarrassment and focus on what you can do to improve and succeed in the future.

So, the next time you face a failure, remember the strategies we have discussed. By seeing the opportunity in failure and approaching it with a positive attitude, you can develop the resilience and determination you need to succeed in life.

A real life example of seeing the opportunity in failure is the story of Thomas Edison. Thomas Edison is well-known for inventing the light bulb, but what many people don't know is that he failed thousands of times before he finally succeeded.

At first, Edison was frustrated by his failures and felt discouraged. But, instead of giving up, he reframed his failures as opportunities to learn. He looked at each failure as a step closer to success, and used what he learned from each failure to make improvements and try again.

Edison once famously said, "I have not failed. I've just found 10,000 ways that won't work." This attitude helped him persevere through the many challenges he faced, and eventually led to his greatest success: the invention of the light bulb.

So, like Edison, we can learn to see the opportunity in failure. By approaching challenges with a positive attitude and a growth mindset, we can develop resilience, determination, and the skills we need to succeed in life.

Another real life example of seeing the opportunity in failure is the story of Walt Disney. Walt Disney's first animation studio, Laugh-O-Gram, went bankrupt in 1923. This could have been a devastating blow, but instead of giving up, Disney saw the opportunity in failure.

He moved to Hollywood and started a new studio, which eventually became the Walt Disney Company. Over the years, Disney faced many challenges and setbacks, but he never lost sight of his dream. He continued to work hard and persevere, eventually creating some of the most beloved characters and stories of all time.

Disney once said, "All the adversity I've had in my life, all my troubles and obstacles, have strengthened me... You may not realize it when it happens, but a kick in the teeth may be the best thing in the world for you." This positive attitude helped him overcome obstacles and achieve great success.

So, just like Walt Disney, we can learn to see the opportunity in failure. By embracing challenges and working hard, we can develop the determination and resilience we need to achieve our dreams.

Another key aspect of seeing the opportunity in failure is to view mistakes as a source of growth and learning. When we make a mistake, we have the chance to reflect on what went wrong and figure out how we can do better next time. This type of self-reflection and improvement is a critical life skill, as it helps us to become better versions of ourselves.

It is also important to remember that failure is a normal part of the learning process. No one is perfect, and everyone makes mistakes. When we can acknowledge and accept that failure is a normal part of life, it becomes easier to see the opportunity in it.

Moreover, seeing the opportunity in failure also requires a growth mindset. Instead of seeing failures as permanent and insurmountable, we can view them as temporary and solvable. This mindset shift can help us to overcome challenges and see the positive aspects of our experiences.

In conclusion, by embracing failure and viewing it as a learning opportunity, we can develop the resilience, determination, and self-reflection skills we need to grow and succeed in life. So, whenever you encounter a setback or mistake, try to see the opportunity in it and use it as a chance to grow and learn.

Making Sound Choices

Making good decisions is a critical life skill that helps us navigate the challenges and choices we face every day. Whether we are deciding what to eat for breakfast or choosing a career path, the ability to make thoughtful and well-informed decisions is essential to our success and happiness.

In this chapter, we will explore the key elements of good decision making and learn how to use these skills to make better choices in our lives. We will learn about the importance of setting clear goals, considering our options, weighing the pros and cons, and making choices that align with our values and priorities.

It is also important to understand that good decision making is not just about making the right choice, but also about taking responsibility for the decisions we make. This means being accountable for the consequences of our choices and using our experiences, both positive and negative, to inform our future decisions.

One of the most important skills in decision making is the ability to think critically. This means considering all the available information and evaluating it in a logical and systematic way. When we think critically, we are better able to make informed and well-reasoned decisions that are in our best interests.

Finally, it is important to remember that good decision making is a process and not a one-time event. Whether we are making small daily choices or major life decisions, we can always strive to improve our decision-making skills and make the best choices for ourselves and those around us.

So, let's start our journey to better decision making and learn how to make choices that lead to a happy, healthy, and successful life.

Don't Select An Option

When faced with a difficult decision, it can be tempting to just avoid making a choice altogether. This may seem like the easiest option, but in reality, not making a choice is still making a choice. When we don't make a decision, we are letting someone else or something else make the decision for us, which can have negative consequences.

For example, imagine you are faced with choosing what to eat for lunch. If you don't make a choice, your hunger will eventually make the decision for you, and you may end up grabbing unhealthy junk food instead of a healthy meal. Or, if you're faced with a tough school assignment, not making a decision means that you're choosing to not complete the assignment and potentially receiving a poor grade.

It's important to remember that making no choice is still a choice, and that it can lead to negative consequences. So, instead of avoiding decisions, it's best to take the time to evaluate your options and make an informed choice. This will help you feel in control and lead to better outcomes.

Making no choice can sometimes be the best choice. This might sound strange, but there are times when not making a decision can actually lead to better outcomes than making a decision.

For example, let's say you are at the mall with your family and you are faced with the decision of whether to buy a new toy or not. You really want the toy, but you also know that you should save your money for something more important. In this situation, making no choice and not buying the toy is the better decision.

Another example is when you are faced with a difficult decision at school. Maybe you are torn between two different projects to work on. Instead of making a choice right away, take some time to think about it and weigh the pros and cons of each option. This way, you can make a better informed decision and avoid making a mistake.

In conclusion, making no choice can be a wise decision when faced with tough choices or decisions that require careful consideration. Remember, taking your time and making a well thought out decision is always better than rushing into something and regretting it later.

Deciding Without Thinking

It's easy to make decisions without thinking when you're caught up in the moment. You might see something you really want and impulsively buy it, or make a choice in the heat of the moment without considering the consequences. However, making choices without thinking can lead to regret and can make it difficult to achieve your goals.

To avoid making choices without thinking, it's important to take a step back and evaluate the situation. Ask yourself some questions like: "Do I need this?", "What will happen if I buy this?", "What are the consequences of this choice?" This can help you make informed decisions that are in line with your values and goals.

Another way to avoid making choices without thinking is to slow down and take your time. Take a deep breath, count to 10, or go for a walk to clear your head. This can help you make more thoughtful decisions and avoid impulsiveness.

It's also important to consider your values and priorities when making decisions. What is most important to you? What do you want to achieve in life? When you make choices that align with your values and priorities, you're more likely to feel confident and happy with your decisions.

In conclusion, making choices without thinking can lead to regret and can make it difficult to achieve your goals. To avoid this, it's important to take a step back, evaluate the situation, slow down, and consider your values and priorities. By making informed, thoughtful decisions, you can achieve your goals and live a life that's true to who you are.

Making Prudent Decisions

Making decisions is an important part of growing up and becoming more independent. But, not all decisions are created equal. Some are quick and simple, while others are more complex and require more thought. In this subchapter, we will explore the importance of thoughtful decision making and how it can help you make the best choices for yourself.

Thoughtful decision making means taking the time to consider all the options available to you, weighing the pros and cons of each, and ultimately making a choice based on what you believe is best for you. It requires paying attention to your own needs, values, and goals, as well as considering the needs and opinions of others.

A good way to start the decision making process is by asking yourself some important questions. What are your goals? What are your values? What do you want to achieve? Answering these questions can help you narrow down your options and make the best choice.

Another important aspect of thoughtful decision making is considering the consequences of each option. What will happen if you choose one option over another? Will it bring you closer to your goals or further away? Will it make you happy or unhappy? Will it impact others in a positive or negative way?

Finally, it's important to be open to change and willing to adapt your decision if new information comes to light. Life is constantly changing, and the best decision for you today may not be the best decision for you tomorrow. By being flexible and open-minded, you can make the best choices for yourself, no matter what life throws your way.

By following these steps, you can make thoughtful decisions that are in line with your goals, values, and needs. And, when you make decisions this way, you'll feel more confident, empowered, and in control of your life.

Thoughtful decision making is a process where you take the time to consider all the options and consequences before making a choice. This type of decision making is important because it helps you make the best possible decision for your situation. To make thoughtful decisions, you need to follow these steps:

Identify the problem: The first step is to identify what the problem is and what you need to make a decision about.

Gather information: Look for information and data that will help you understand the problem better. This could include talking to others, researching online, or reading books.

Consider options: Once you have all the information, think about all the possible options for solving the problem. List them out and think about the pros and cons of each one.

Make a decision: After you've considered all the options, make a decision about which one you think is the best. Make sure to consider the potential consequences of each choice before making your final decision.

Take action: The final step is to take action and put your decision into action. Remember, this is not the end of the process. Keep an eye on the results and be prepared to adjust your decision if necessary.

For example, let's say your best friend invited you to play video games all day instead of doing your homework. A thoughtful decision making process would involve considering the consequences of skipping your homework, such as lower grades, and the importance of keeping up with your responsibilities. You could then make a decision to do your homework first, and then have time to play video games later.

Remember, making thoughtful decisions takes time and effort, but it will help you make the best choices for your future.

The Right Mindset For Prosperity

One of the keys to a happy and fulfilling life is having a positive and prosperous mindset. When we have the right mindset, we can overcome challenges and reach our goals, no matter how big or small they may be. In this chapter, we'll talk about how you can develop a prosperous mindset, so you can live a life full of happiness, success, and prosperity.

A prosperous mindset is not just about having money, it's about having a positive attitude and outlook on life. When you have a prosperous mindset, you see opportunities instead of obstacles, and you're able to turn your dreams into reality. You also develop a growth mindset, which means you believe that you can always learn and grow, and that challenges are just opportunities for growth.

To develop a prosperous mindset, it's important to focus on your thoughts and beliefs. Our thoughts and beliefs shape our reality, so if we want to live a prosperous life, we need to have positive and productive thoughts and beliefs. Here are some tips to help you develop a prosperous mindset:

Focus on gratitude: Take time each day to reflect on the things you're grateful for in your life. When we focus on what we have, instead of what we don't have, it helps us have a more positive outlook on life.

Surround yourself with positive people: Being around people who have a positive and prosperous mindset will help you develop a prosperous mindset too. Surrounding yourself with positive and supportive people will help you see the world in a more positive light.

Practice visualization: Visualize yourself having all the things you want in life. See yourself happy, successful, and prosperous, and focus on that vision every day.

Take action: It's important to take action towards your goals, but it's also important to enjoy the journey. Celebrate your small victories along the way, and remember that every step forward is a step closer to your goals.

By following these tips, you'll be well on your way to developing a prosperous mindset, and living a happy and fulfilling life. Remember, your thoughts and beliefs shape your reality, so focus on positive and productive thoughts, and you'll be able to turn your dreams into reality.

Keep Your Positivity

Staying positive is a critical life skill that will help you succeed and be happy in life. This subchapter will help you understand why staying positive is important and how you can develop a positive mindset.

Why is staying positive important?

Having a positive mindset can help you:

Face challenges with confidence

Attract positive experiences and people into your life

Handle negative situations more effectively

Increase your resilience and overall well-being

How can you stay positive?

Here are some tips for developing and maintaining a positive mindset:

Practice gratitude: Take time each day to think about and write down things you're thankful for. This will help shift your focus from negative to positive thoughts.

Surround yourself with positive people: Seek out friends, family members, and other people who are supportive and have a positive outlook on life.

Find joy in simple things: Take pleasure in the little things in life, like a beautiful sunset or spending time with friends.

Focus on the present moment: Avoid dwelling on the past or worrying about the future. Instead, focus on the present and what you can do right now to feel good.

Take care of your physical health: Exercise regularly, eat well, and get enough sleep. Taking care of your body can help improve your mood and overall well-being.

In conclusion, staying positive is a valuable life skill that will help you navigate challenges and be successful and happy. By practicing gratitude, surrounding yourself with positive people, finding joy in simple things, focusing on the present, and taking care of your physical health, you can develop and maintain a positive mindset.

Staying positive is a key factor in having a prosperous life. When faced with challenges or obstacles, it can be easy to fall into a negative mindset and lose hope. However, it's important to remember that your thoughts and attitudes have a significant impact on your experiences and outcomes. Keeping a positive outlook can help you see opportunities where others see only problems and can give you the motivation and energy you need to tackle any challenge that comes your way.

One way to cultivate a positive mindset is to surround yourself with positive influences. This can mean seeking out people who lift you up, listening to uplifting music, reading inspiring books, and engaging in activities that bring you joy. Additionally, it's important to practice gratitude and take time to acknowledge and appreciate the good things in your life, no matter how small they may seem.

Another helpful technique is to reframe negative thoughts. When you catch yourself thinking negatively, try to find a more positive way to look at the situation. For example, instead of thinking "I'll never be able to do this", try to think "I'm still learning and I'll get better with practice". These small shifts in perspective can make a big difference in how you feel and approach challenges.

Finally, it's important to be kind to yourself and not be too hard on yourself when things

A real-life example of staying positive can be seen in the story of a young girl named Sarah. Sarah loved to play basketball, but she wasn't very good at it. Every time she missed a shot or made a mistake during a game, she would get upset and discouraged.

One day, Sarah's coach sat her down and told her that the most important thing was to stay positive, no matter what. The coach told Sarah to focus on the things she did well, instead of dwelling on her mistakes.

Sarah took the coach's advice to heart, and started to think more positively. Every time she missed a shot, she would say to herself, "That's okay, I'll get the next one." She also started to focus on the things she did well, like getting a steal or making a great pass.

As Sarah started to focus on the positive, she began to improve as a player. She was making more shots, playing better defense, and having more fun on the court. By staying positive, Sarah was able to become a better basketball player and enjoy the game more.

This story shows how staying positive can help you overcome challenges and reach your goals. By focusing on the good things, and not getting discouraged by mistakes, you can stay motivated and make progress in anything you do.

Setting Your Goals

Goal setting is a powerful tool that can help you reach your dreams and aspirations. It's a way to clarify what you want to achieve and to put a plan in place to make it happen. In this subchapter, you will learn how to set and achieve your goals, no matter how big or small they may be.

First, think about what you would like to achieve. It can be anything from learning a new skill, to getting good grades, to saving money. The important thing is that the goal is something you truly want and that it inspires you.

Next, make your goal specific and measurable. Instead of simply saying, "I want to be good at sports," say, "I want to improve my basketball skills and score an average of 10 points per game by the end of the season." This way, you have a clear target to work towards.

Write down your goal and put it somewhere where you will see it every day. This will keep you motivated and focused.

Now, make a plan of action. Break your goal down into smaller, manageable steps and set deadlines for each step. For example, if your goal is to improve your basketball skills, your plan of action might include practicing every day, attending a basketball camp, and watching videos of successful basketball players to learn from them.

Finally, keep track of your progress. Celebrate each step you take towards your goal and adjust your plan if necessary. Remember, goal setting is a journey, not a destination. It's about constantly learning and growing, so don't be discouraged if things don't go exactly as planned.

A real life example of goal setting could be a child who wants to learn how to play the piano. The child sets a goal to play a song on the piano by the end of the year. The child then breaks down this goal into smaller steps, such as practicing every day for 30 minutes, taking lessons once a week, and listening to piano music to get inspired. By following this plan and celebrating their progress along the way, the child can reach their goal of playing a song on the piano.

Goal setting is an important life skill that can help children achieve their dreams and aspirations. This subchapter will help kids understand the benefits of setting goals and how to do it effectively.

The first step in goal setting is to identify what a child wants to achieve. This could be anything from getting good grades in school to learning a new sport or hobby. Once the goal has been identified, it is important to break it down into smaller, achievable steps. This will help the child see progress along the way and feel a sense of accomplishment as they work towards their goal.

Another important aspect of goal setting is to establish a timeline for each step. This could be a specific date or deadline that the child works towards. Having a timeline will help them stay focused and motivated.

It's also important to make a plan for how the child will achieve each step of their goal. This could involve creating a list of tasks that need to be completed, or setting up a schedule to practice a new sport or hobby. Having a plan in place will help the child stay organized and focused on their goal.

Finally, it's important to encourage kids to stay positive and to keep pushing forward, even when they face challenges. Remind them that setbacks and failures are a natural part of the process and that success is not achieved overnight. With hard work and determination, they can reach their goals.

Giving real-life examples of successful people who set goals and worked towards them can be a great way to inspire kids to set their own. For example, a famous athlete who set a goal to win a gold medal and trained every day to achieve it, or a young inventor who set a goal to create a new invention and worked tirelessly to make it a reality. These examples can help kids understand the power of goal setting and inspire them to pursue their own dreams.

Talk And Listen

Good communication skills are a crucial part of life and can help you in many different ways. Whether you're talking to friends, family, or teachers, having the ability to express yourself clearly and effectively can make a big difference in your relationships and success.

In this chapter, we'll be exploring the importance of communication and some of the key elements that make up effective communication. We'll also be looking at different types of communication and the different ways you can use them to get your message across.

So, why is communication so important? Well, for starters, it allows you to build strong relationships with others. When you communicate well, people are more likely to understand you, trust you, and respect you. Good communication can also help you resolve conflicts and make better decisions, both in your personal life and in the wider world.

So, how do you become a great communicator? It starts with understanding the different components of communication, including body language, tone of voice, and the words you choose to use. All of these elements work together to help you get your message across and make sure it is understood.

In this chapter, we'll be diving deeper into some of these elements, looking at how they can be used to improve your communication skills and help you connect with others in a meaningful way. So, whether you're an introvert or an extrovert, whether you're shy or confident, communication is a skill that anyone can learn and improve. Let's get started!

One example of how kids can develop good communication skills is by practicing active listening. This means paying attention to what the other person is saying, making eye contact, and responding in a way that shows you understand. Kids can practice this by having conversations with family members, friends, or even their pets!

Another way to improve communication skills is by expressing themselves clearly and concisely, using words that are appropriate for their age and audience. Kids can also work on using body language and tone of voice to communicate their message effectively.

For example, speaking loudly and confidently can show that you are confident and assertive, while speaking softly and hesitantly can suggest that you are unsure or not confident. Encouraging kids to participate in group activities or team sports can also help them build their communication skills, as they learn how to work with others, negotiate, and share their thoughts and ideas.

In order to continue developing good communication skills, kids can practice active listening. This means giving their full attention to the person speaking and trying to understand their perspective. It's also important to ask questions to clarify what the speaker is saying, and to show that they are interested in what they have to say. Additionally, kids can work on expressing themselves clearly and effectively, using appropriate body language, tone, and word choice. This can be done by participating in class discussions, giving presentations, and practicing talking to others in various social situations.

Another aspect of good communication is being able to resolve conflicts effectively. Kids can learn how to approach a disagreement in a calm and respectful manner, and to find a solution that works for everyone. They can also learn how to apologize when they have made a mistake, and how to forgive others for their mistakes.

Good communication is also about being able to understand and respect the feelings of others. Kids can work on developing empathy, which means trying to put themselves in other people's shoes and understanding how they feel. This can help them build stronger relationships and be more effective communicators in all aspects of their life.

Body language is a powerful tool that can greatly impact the way we communicate with others. It's estimated that around 60-70% of our communication is conveyed through nonverbal cues like gestures, facial expressions, and posture. Understanding how our body language affects communication can help kids become more effective communicators and build stronger relationships.

For example, when we smile, we convey warmth and friendliness, making others feel at ease and more likely to trust us. On the other hand, crossed arms or a furrowed brow can signal defensiveness or disapproval, which can make others feel less comfortable and less likely to listen. Eye contact is another important aspect of body language. When we look someone in the eye, we show that we are engaged, attentive, and trustworthy. However, if we avoid eye contact, it can signal disinterest or dishonesty.

By being aware of their own body language, kids can learn to use it to their advantage, making them better communicators. Additionally, by observing the body language of others, kids can gain valuable insights into how others are feeling and what they might be thinking, which can help them navigate social situations more effectively.

In conclusion, body language is a critical component of communication, and it's never too early for kids to start learning how to use it effectively. By teaching them the power of body language and how to read the cues of others, they can become confident communicators and build stronger relationships with those around them.

Listening is one of the key components of effective communication. Good listening skills can help individuals understand others' perspectives, feelings, and ideas, and also show respect and care. When we listen, we pay attention to what the speaker is saying and try to understand their message.

For kids, learning to listen effectively can help them in various situations, such as in the classroom, with friends and family, or even in conflict resolution. When kids listen, they can gather important information and make better decisions, as well as build stronger relationships with others.

Effective listening also involves avoiding distractions and maintaining eye contact with the speaker. When we are distracted, we may miss important details or misinterpret what is being said. Additionally, maintaining eye contact with the speaker shows that we are paying attention and interested in what they have to say.

Another important aspect of listening is asking questions. Asking questions shows that we are engaged in the conversation and want to learn more about the topic. This can also help to clarify any misunderstandings and can improve the flow of the conversation.

In conclusion, listening is a critical component of effective communication, and kids can benefit greatly from developing good listening skills. By paying attention, avoiding distractions, maintaining eye contact, and asking questions, kids can build stronger relationships and make better decisions.

Keeping Calm In A Case Of Need

Emergencies can happen at any time, and it's essential to know how to stay calm and composed when they do. When you're prepared, you're more likely to handle an emergency effectively, which can save lives and prevent further harm. This chapter will help you develop the skills you need to keep your cool in an emergency.

When an emergency occurs, it's natural to feel scared, confused, or overwhelmed. However, it's essential to remain calm and focus on what needs to be done. In an emergency situation, every second counts, and panicking can waste precious time.

The first step to keeping your cool in an emergency is to be prepared. Make sure you know what to do in case of an emergency, and have a plan in place. For example, if there's a fire in your home, know the quickest way to get out and have a designated meeting spot outside. If you're in a public place, know the location of the nearest exits, and identify any potential hazards.

Another critical skill for handling emergencies is to remain level-headed. Take a deep breath and assess the situation. Think about what needs to be done, and act quickly but calmly. Remember, if you panic, you're more likely to make mistakes, and those mistakes could have serious consequences.

It's also crucial to stay focused and to communicate clearly. In an emergency, it's easy to become distracted or to misunderstand instructions. Be sure to listen carefully to what's being said and ask questions if you're unsure. If you're in a group, assign tasks to each person, and make sure everyone knows what they need to do.

Finally, remember that emergencies can be traumatic and emotional experiences. It's important to take care of yourself and those around you after an emergency has occurred. Be sure to reach out to loved ones for support, and seek professional help if needed.

By being prepared, staying level-headed, and communicating effectively, you can keep your cool in an emergency and help ensure the safety of yourself and others.

How To Do An Emergency Call

Emergencies can happen at any time, and it is important to know how to respond to them. One of the most important skills you can have is knowing how to call 911. 911 is the emergency phone number that you can call if there is an emergency that requires immediate attention from the police, firefighters, or medical personnel.

Here are the steps you can follow to call 911:

Step 1: Stay Calm The first thing to do when you need to call 911 is to stay calm. Take a deep breath and try to keep your voice steady. This will help the person on the other end of the line understand you clearly.

Step 2: Dial 911 Next, pick up the phone and dial 911. The operator will answer the phone and ask, "911, what is your emergency?" You will then need to tell them what the emergency is and where you are. It is important to give your location first so that the emergency responders can find you quickly.

Step 3: Explain the Emergency Once you have given your location, explain the emergency in as much detail as possible. If someone is injured, describe their injuries and if they are conscious or not. If there is a fire, describe where the fire is and if anyone is trapped. If someone is breaking into your home, describe what they look like and what they are doing.

Step 4: Follow the Operator's Instructions The operator will then give you instructions on what to do next. They may ask you to stay on the line or to do something to help the person in need. It is important to follow the operator's instructions carefully.

Step 5: Stay Calm and Wait for Help Stay on the line with the operator until help arrives. The operator may ask you to perform first aid or CPR if necessary, but only do so if you are trained to do so.

Remember, calling 911 is for emergencies only. It is important to use this service responsibly and only call if there is a real emergency. False alarms can put other people's lives in danger, and emergency services are stretched thin enough as it is.

In conclusion, knowing how to call 911 can save lives in an emergency. It is a simple but important skill to have, and it is important to stay calm and follow the operator's instructions when you make the call.

How To Transmit Information

When you are in an emergency situation, it is very important to relay information to the emergency responders clearly and effectively. This subchapter will provide you with some helpful tips on how to do just that.

The first step in relaying information is to remain calm. Take a deep breath and try to keep a clear head. This will help you to remember important details and communicate them effectively.

The next step is to make sure you provide accurate information. Tell the emergency responders exactly what is happening and where it is happening. For example, if there is a fire, let them know the location of the fire, how big it is, and whether anyone is trapped inside the building.

When giving information, speak clearly and slowly. Remember, the emergency responders may be dealing with a lot of different situations at once, so you want to make sure they can understand you clearly. Also, try to avoid using any slang or jargon that they may not understand.

If you are not sure about any details, it is okay to say so. The emergency responders would rather you give them accurate information, even if it takes a little longer to get all the facts straight.

Finally, make sure you stay on the line until the emergency responders tell you it is okay to hang up. They may need to ask you additional questions or give you further instructions, so it is important to remain available until they tell you otherwise.

Remember, relaying information is a key part of staying safe in an emergency situation. By following these tips, you can help ensure that you are providing accurate and useful information to the emergency responders, and increase the chances of a positive outcome.

Your Private Data

In an emergency, it is important to be able to quickly and accurately provide your personal information to first responders. This information can include your full name, date of birth, and address. It can also include any medical conditions or medications you are taking, allergies, and emergency contact information.

To make sure you are prepared in case of an emergency, it is a good idea to have this information written down in a safe and easily accessible place. Some families choose to keep this information on a sheet of paper posted in a visible location, like on the fridge or in a central location in the house.

It is also important to know when to share your personal information. While it is important to provide your information in an emergency situation, it is also important to protect your personal information in everyday situations. For example, you should never share your personal information online or with strangers, even if they claim to be from a legitimate organization.

Remember, your personal information is important and should be treated with care. Knowing what information to share, when to share it, and who to share it with can help keep you safe in an emergency and in everyday life.

Tasks Simplify Your Life

As you grow up, it is important to learn how to take care of yourself and your surroundings. One way to do this is by doing chores. Chores are tasks that need to be done to keep your home clean, tidy and organized. It is important to do them regularly and consistently, as this will make your life easier in the long run.

Chores can be divided into different categories such as cleaning, organizing, and maintaining. Cleaning chores include tasks such as washing the dishes, sweeping the floors, and doing laundry. Organizing chores involve tasks such as putting away toys, clothes, and other belongings in their proper places. Maintaining chores include tasks such as watering plants and taking out the trash.

It may seem like a lot of work to do chores, but they have many benefits. First, doing chores teaches you responsibility and independence. When you do chores, you are taking care of yourself and your home. This is an important life skill that you will need as you grow up.

Second, doing chores teaches you time management skills. By setting aside time each day or each week to do chores, you will learn how to manage your time and prioritize tasks. This skill will be useful as you start to take on more responsibilities in your life.

Third, doing chores teaches you how to work as a team. When everyone in your home helps out with chores, it creates a sense of teamwork and collaboration. It also ensures that everyone shares the responsibility of keeping the home clean and organized.

To make chores more manageable and fun, you can create a chore chart or schedule. This can help you keep track of what needs to be done and when. You can also make chores more enjoyable by listening to music or working with a partner.

In conclusion, chores are an important part of taking care of yourself and your home. They teach responsibility, time management, and teamwork. By doing chores regularly and consistently, you will make your life easier and more organized. So, grab a broom, put on some music, and get cleaning!

Tasks Are Learning Possibilities

You might think that chores are boring and just another thing that you have to do, but did you know that they can actually help you learn and grow as a person? That's right! Doing chores can teach you lots of important skills that will come in handy later in life.

One of the most important things that doing chores can teach you is responsibility. When you have a chore to do, it's up to you to make sure that you get it done. You have to take responsibility for your task and make sure that you complete it on time and to the best of your ability. This is a skill that will be very important when you get older and have to take care of yourself.

Another thing that chores can teach you is how to work as a team. If you have siblings, you might have to work together to get all of your chores done. This can help you learn how to cooperate with others and get things done more efficiently. When you're older, you'll be working with lots of different people, and being able to work well with others is an important skill to have.

Chores can also teach you about time management. When you have a list of chores to do, you have to figure out the best way to get them all done in a certain amount of time. This can help you learn how to prioritize your tasks and manage your time effectively. This is a skill that will be very useful when you have a job and other responsibilities to take care of.

In addition to these skills, doing chores can also help you learn about different aspects of life. For example, if you have to do laundry, you'll learn about how to wash and fold clothes. If you have to clean the kitchen, you'll learn about different cleaning products and techniques. These are all things that will be useful to know as you grow up and become more independent.

So, the next time your parents ask you to do a chore, remember that it's not just something that you have to do. It's also an opportunity to learn and grow as a person. Embrace the opportunity to take on responsibilities, work as a team, manage your time, and learn new things. These are all important skills that will help you succeed in life.

Exercise Autonomy

Having the ability to make decisions for ourselves is known as autonomy. In this subchapter, we will learn how doing chores can teach us how to exercise autonomy.

When we do chores, we are given the responsibility to complete a task without being told what to do every step of the way. This means we have to figure out how to complete the task on our own. This can be difficult at first, but with practice, we learn how to make our own decisions.

As we complete our chores, we also learn how to prioritize tasks and make decisions on what to do first. We learn to think critically and to make decisions that make the most sense for the situation.

One way to exercise autonomy when doing chores is by setting goals for ourselves. For example, if we have to clean our room, we can set a goal to complete the task within a certain time frame or to clean every corner of the room. This helps us to take charge of the task and feel proud of our accomplishments.

Another way to exercise autonomy is by being creative in the way we complete our chores. For example, instead of folding our clothes the same way every time, we can try new ways to fold them. This helps us to think outside the box and find new and better ways of doing things.

By exercising autonomy, we learn to make our own decisions and become more independent. This helps us in all aspects of our lives, from school to our future careers.

In conclusion, doing chores is a great way to exercise autonomy and learn how to make our own decisions. By setting goals for ourselves and being creative in the way we complete our chores, we become more independent and better at decision-making.

When you do your chores independently, you get to exercise your autonomy. Autonomy means having control over your own actions and making decisions for yourself. When you take ownership of your chores, you get to decide when and how to do them. This can make you feel more independent and self-sufficient.

For instance, when you're responsible for cleaning your room, you get to decide when to do it, how to organize it, and where to put your stuff. You can also decide whether you want to work on your room alone or with help from someone else. This sense of control can be empowering and make you feel more grown-up.

Moreover, taking ownership of your chores can teach you valuable life skills such as time management, planning, prioritization, and organization. You'll learn to manage your time and work efficiently to complete your chores while also keeping up with other activities like schoolwork, hobbies, and spending time with friends.

Furthermore, when you complete your chores independently, you get to see the results of your efforts. You'll feel proud of yourself when you see your clean room or when you have prepared a meal for your family. This will give you a sense of accomplishment, which can boost your self-esteem and confidence.

In conclusion, exercising autonomy by completing your chores independently has numerous benefits. It can teach you valuable life skills, make you feel more independent, and give you a sense of accomplishment.

Time Management

Time is a precious commodity, and learning how to manage it wisely can make a big difference in how much we can accomplish in a day. Good time management skills can help us achieve our goals and have more time for fun activities. In this chapter, we will explore the basics of time management and how to develop this important life skill.

Prioritizing

When we have a lot of things to do, it can be overwhelming to know where to start. Prioritizing our tasks can help us focus on what is most important and manage our time more effectively. To prioritize, we need to think about what needs to be done first and what can wait.

One way to prioritize is to make a to-do list. Start by writing down all the tasks that need to be done, then number them in order of importance. This can help us focus on what needs to be done first and avoid wasting time on less important tasks.

Breaking Tasks into Manageable Chunks

Big tasks can seem daunting and overwhelming, and it can be hard to know where to start. Breaking tasks down into smaller, more manageable chunks can help us tackle them more easily.

For example, if we need to clean our room, we can break it down into smaller tasks, such as making the bed, putting away clothes, and vacuuming. This can make the task feel less overwhelming and more manageable.

Avoiding Procrastination

Procrastination is the enemy of good time management. When we put off tasks, they can pile up and become even more overwhelming. Learning how to avoid procrastination can help us manage our time more effectively.

One way to avoid procrastination is to set a specific time for each task on our to-do list. This can help us stay focused and avoid getting sidetracked. Another strategy is to break a big task into smaller, more manageable chunks and give ourselves a deadline for each one.

In conclusion, time management is an important life skill that can help us be more productive and achieve our goals. By prioritizing our tasks, breaking them down into smaller chunks, and avoiding procrastination, we can make the most of our time and enjoy our lives to the fullest.

Set Priorities

Do you ever feel like you have too much to do and not enough time to do it all? It can be overwhelming, but learning how to prioritize can help you manage your time better.

Prioritizing means deciding what is most important and doing those things first. You can start by making a list of all the things you need to do. Then, think about which tasks are the most important or have a deadline coming up soon. Those are the tasks you should focus on first.

For example, if you have a big project due for school next week, it's important to prioritize working on that project over playing video games. You can still play video games, but it's important to focus on the most important tasks first.

Remember, it's okay to ask for help if you need it. If you're having trouble prioritizing, ask a parent or teacher for advice. They might be able to help you see things more clearly and come up with a plan.

Learning to prioritize is an important skill that can help you not only manage your time better, but also reduce stress and feel more in control of your life. With practice, you'll become a pro at prioritizing and be able to get more done in less time.

Generating a Routine

As humans, we all have different natural rhythms, and we work best when we have a consistent routine. A routine is a schedule or a set of habits that you do at the same time every day or on certain days of the week. When you have a routine, you can organize your time better and get more things done.

Developing a routine takes time and effort, but it's worth it. When you have a routine, you know what to expect each day. You won't have to worry about what you need to do next or forget important tasks.

Here are some tips on how to develop a routine:

Start small: When you're first starting out, it's important to start small. Don't try to change everything at once. Pick one or two things that you want to add to your routine, and focus on them. Once those habits become second nature, you can add more.

Write it down: Write down your routine so that you can see it. It's easier to follow a routine when you can see it in front of you.

Stick to a schedule: Decide on a set time for each activity and stick to it. For example, you might decide to wake up at 6:30 a.m., eat breakfast at 7:00 a.m., and start your homework at 7:30 a.m. If you stick to your schedule, your routine will become a habit.

Make time for what's important: Make sure you include time for the things that are important to you in your routine. For example, if spending time with your family is important to you, make sure you include that in your routine.

Be flexible: Your routine should be flexible. Don't be afraid to adjust your routine if it's not working for you. Life happens, and sometimes you need to be able to change your routine to accommodate unexpected events.

By developing a routine, you'll be able to manage your time better and get more things done. With practice and consistency, your routine will become a habit, and you'll be on your way to better time management.

Monetary Consciousness

Money is an important part of life. We need money to buy things we want and need. Financial awareness means understanding how money works and learning how to make the most of the money we have.

<u>Earning Money</u>

One way to get money is by earning it. You can earn money by doing jobs like mowing lawns, walking dogs, or helping with chores around the house. You can also earn money by doing tasks for others or selling things you make.

It's important to remember that when you earn money, you should save some of it too. Saving money means putting it away for later. This can be helpful if you need money for an emergency or if you want to buy something big in the future.

<u>Spending Money Wisely</u>

When you have money, it's important to spend it wisely. This means thinking carefully about what you want to buy and deciding if it's something you really need or just something you want.

One way to make sure you're spending money wisely is by making a budget. A budget is a plan that helps you keep track of how much money you have and how much you can spend. When you make a budget, you can decide how much money you want to save and how much you want to spend on things like food, clothes, and toys.

<u>Giving Back</u>

Another important part of financial awareness is learning how to give back. Giving back means using some of your money or time to help others. You can donate money to a charity or volunteer at a local organization.

Giving back can be a great way to make a difference in your community and feel good about yourself. It can also teach you the value of helping others and how it can make a positive impact on the world.

In conclusion, financial awareness is an important skill that can help you make the most of the money you have. By earning money, spending it wisely, and giving back, you can develop good habits that will benefit you throughout your life.

Managing money and making wise financial decisions is important at any age, even for kids. Understanding the value of money, saving for the future, and spending responsibly are skills that can be learned and practiced over time. By developing good financial habits early in life, kids can set themselves up for success in the future.

<u>Budgeting</u>

One important concept to teach kids about is budgeting. This means making a plan for how to spend and save money. Start by explaining the difference between needs and wants. Needs are things that are necessary for survival, like food, shelter, and clothing. Wants are things that we desire but can live without, like toys, gadgets, and treats. Help your child make a list of their needs and wants, and work together to figure out how to allocate money to each category.

<u>Saving Money</u>

Another important financial skill is saving money. Encourage your child to save a portion of any money they receive, whether it's from an allowance, birthday gifts, or doing chores. Set a savings goal, like saving for a special toy or a future purchase, and help your child track their progress. This will teach them the value of delayed gratification and the importance of having savings for emergencies.

It's also important to teach kids about spending responsibly. Talk to them about the difference between spending money on things that bring long-term value versus things that provide only short-term satisfaction. For example, buying a new book that can be read multiple times versus a piece of candy that's gone after one bite.

Teaching kids about money and financial responsibility may not be easy, but it's an important life skill that will serve them well in the long run. By helping kids develop good financial habits and understanding the value of money, we can help them build a foundation for a secure and prosperous future.

Making Money

Learning about money is an essential life skill that every kid should know. One of the best ways to become financially aware is by learning how to earn money. You don't have to wait until you're an adult to make money. There are many ways kids can earn money and learn important financial lessons along the way.

Allowance: Getting an allowance from your parents or guardians is a great way to earn money. It's usually given weekly or monthly, and it's meant to help you learn how to manage money. You can use your allowance to buy things you want, save for something special, or even donate to charity.

Chores: Doing chores around the house is another way to earn money. Your parents or guardians may pay you for doing things like cleaning your room, washing the dishes, or mowing the lawn. Not only does this teach you the value of hard work, but it also shows you that money is earned through effort.

Yard work: If you live in a neighborhood with lots of houses, you can offer to do yard work for your neighbors. This can include mowing lawns, pulling weeds, or raking leaves. You can charge a reasonable fee and even turn it into a small business by promoting your services to other neighbors.

Selling items: You may have items in your room that you no longer use or need. You can sell them online on websites like eBay or Amazon, or hold a garage sale. This not only earns you money but also teaches you about the value of possessions and the importance of decluttering.

It's important to remember that when earning money, it's also important to save and spend wisely. You should aim to save a portion of your earnings for future expenses or emergencies, and to spend your money on things that are important to you.

In conclusion, earning money is a crucial part of financial awareness. It teaches kids about the value of hard work, saving, and spending wisely. There are many ways to earn money, and by doing so, kids can develop a better understanding of how money works in the real world.

Conserving Your Funds

Saving money is a great habit that can help you achieve your financial goals. When you save money, you set aside some of your earnings for future use. This could be for something you want to buy or for a rainy day. Here are some tips to help you save money:

Set a savings goal: It's important to know what you are saving for. You could save for a toy, a gadget, or something else you really want. When you have a savings goal, you'll be motivated to save more.

Make a budget: A budget is a plan that helps you manage your money. It's important to make a budget that includes your income and expenses. This way, you'll know how much you can save each week or month.

Use a piggy bank or a savings account: You can use a piggy bank to save your money. This is a great way to save small amounts of money. Alternatively, you could open a savings account at a bank. This is a safe place to keep your money, and it earns interest over time.

Avoid impulse buying: Impulse buying is when you buy something on the spur of the moment, without thinking it through. It's important to avoid impulse buying if you want to save money. Before making a purchase, think about whether you really need it.

Find ways to cut back on expenses: There are many ways to cut back on expenses. For example, you could make your own lunch instead of buying it, or turn off the lights when you leave a room. These small changes can add up over time, helping you save more money.

Remember, saving money is a great habit to develop. It helps you achieve your goals and can give you peace of mind knowing you have a safety net for unexpected expenses.

Once you have money, the next step is to save it! Saving money means not spending it all right away, but putting some aside for later. There are many reasons to save money. You might want to save up for something special, like a new bike or a toy. Or, you might want to save up for something important, like college or a down payment on a house.

One way to start saving money is to set a goal. Decide on something you want to save up for and figure out how much money you'll need. Then, come up with a plan for how you'll save that money. You might decide to save a certain amount of money each week or each month, or you might decide to put a percentage of your allowance or earnings into a savings account.

Another way to save money is to look for ways to cut back on your expenses. For example, you might decide to bring your lunch to school instead of buying it, or to turn off the lights and electronics when you're not using them to save on your energy bill. You could also try to find ways to earn more money, like doing extra chores or starting a small business selling things you've made.

Finally, it's important to choose a safe and secure place to keep your savings. You might decide to keep your money in a piggy bank, a savings account at a bank, or a special investment account like a 529 plan for education savings.

Remember, saving money is an important habit to develop early on in life, and it can help set you up for financial success in the future!

Cutting expenses is an important aspect of saving money. This means spending less on things that you don't necessarily need or finding ways to get the things you need for a lower price.

One way to cut expenses is to make a budget. A budget is a plan for how you will spend your money. It's important to make a budget so you can see exactly where your money is going and figure out where you can cut back. For example, you might realize that you're spending a lot of money on snacks or fast food, and decide to start packing your own snacks and meals instead.

Another way to cut expenses is to shop around for deals. Instead of buying the first thing you see, look around for better prices. You can compare prices at different stores or online, or look for coupons and discounts. You might also consider buying used items or borrowing from friends and family instead of buying new.

Cutting expenses doesn't have to be boring or hard. It can be a fun challenge to see how much you can save. And the money you save can go towards more important things, like saving for college or a big purchase, or donating to a charity you care about.

Using Appliances

As children grow up, they learn how to use many different types of appliances. Some appliances, like a toaster or microwave, are easy to use, while others, like a washing machine or vacuum cleaner, might take a bit more practice to learn. It's important to learn how to operate these appliances properly to avoid damaging them or causing harm.

Reading the Instructions

Before using any appliance, it's essential to read the instructions carefully. The instructions will tell you how to use the appliance, any safety precautions you should take, and how to maintain the appliance.

Electrical Safety

Many appliances require electricity to function, and it's essential to use them safely. When plugging in an appliance, make sure that the outlet is not damaged, and the plug is inserted correctly. Do not touch an appliance with wet hands or when standing on a wet surface. It is also essential to unplug appliances when not in use.

Kitchen Appliances

Kitchen appliances, such as the microwave, oven, blender, or mixer, make cooking and baking much easier. However, it's important to understand how to operate them correctly. Always use oven mitts when taking things out of the oven or handling hot pots and pans. Do not put metal or aluminum foil in a microwave, and never leave an appliance unattended while it's in use.

Laundry Appliances

Laundry appliances, such as the washing machine and dryer, can be a bit more complicated to operate. Always sort your laundry by color and fabric type and use the correct amount of detergent. It's also important to clean the lint trap after every use to prevent a fire.

Cleaning Appliances

Cleaning appliances, like the vacuum cleaner or steam mop, can be tricky to use, but they can make cleaning much more manageable. Always check that the vacuum's filter is clean and that there are no blockages before use. Use the correct type of cleaning solution in a steam mop and make sure to follow the instructions for the machine.

Learning how to operate appliances correctly will make your life much easier and safer. Remember to read the instructions carefully, use appliances safely, and maintain them correctly.

How To Utilize The Washing Machine

Using a washing machine can be a little tricky if you have never done it before. However, with the right instructions, it can be easy and fun. Here is a step-by-step guide on how to use a washing machine:

Step 1: Sort Your Clothes

Before washing your clothes, you should sort them according to color and type of fabric. For example, you can put all your whites together and all your darks together. This will prevent the colors from bleeding into each other.

Step 2: Add Detergent

Add the detergent to the dispenser or the drum, depending on the type of washing machine you have. Be careful not to use too much detergent as it can make your clothes soapy and difficult to rinse.

Step 3: Load the Machine

Open the door of the washing machine and place your sorted clothes inside. Be sure not to overfill the machine, as this can affect how well the clothes are cleaned.

Step 4: Choose Your Settings

Select the settings that correspond to the type of clothes you are washing. For example, if you are washing delicate fabrics, choose the delicate cycle. Also, choose the right water temperature for your clothes. Hot water is good for removing stains and dirt, while cold water is best for delicate clothes.

Step 5: Start the Washing Machine

Once you have selected the settings, close the door and start the machine. You can sit back and relax while the washing machine does the work.

Step 6: Dry Your Clothes

After the washing cycle is complete, you can transfer your clothes to the dryer. If you don't have a dryer, you can hang your clothes to dry outside or inside your house.

Remember to always clean your washing machine after every use to avoid the buildup of detergent and dirt. You can wipe the drum and the exterior of the machine with a damp cloth.

Using a washing machine is not only fun, but it can also save you time and energy. With these simple steps, you can wash your clothes like a pro.

How To Use The Dishwasher

Do you ever feel like washing dishes by hand is a never-ending task? Luckily, there's a machine that can make your life much easier - the dishwasher! Here's how you can use it:

Load the dishwasher: Open the dishwasher and put in all of the dirty dishes. Make sure that nothing is blocking the spinning arms or spray nozzles. Also, don't forget to remove any leftover food from the dishes, as this can clog the machine.

Add detergent: Depending on the type of detergent you're using, you may need to put it in a specific compartment or just sprinkle it over the dishes. Follow the instructions on the detergent container to make sure you use the right amount.

Choose a cycle: Different dishwashers have different cycle options, such as normal, quick, or heavy. Select the cycle that's appropriate for your dishes and the level of dirt.
Turn on the dishwasher: Once you've loaded the dishwasher and added detergent, close the door and press the "start" button. The dishwasher will begin to clean the dishes.

Unload the dishwasher: After the cycle is complete, the dishwasher will make a sound to let you know that it's finished. Open the dishwasher and remove the clean dishes. Make sure that they are completely dry before putting them away.

It's important to note that not all dishes can go in the dishwasher. Some materials, such as wood or cast iron, should be washed by hand. Additionally, certain dishes may not be dishwasher-safe, so be sure to check the manufacturer's instructions.

Using a dishwasher is a great way to save time and make your life easier. Just remember to load it correctly, use the right detergent and cycle, and always unload the clean dishes when the cycle is complete.

Here are some additional points to consider when using the dishwasher:

Load the dishwasher correctly: Make sure you load the dishwasher properly to ensure that your dishes come out clean. Place large items such as pots and pans on the bottom rack, and smaller items such as glasses and bowls on the top rack. Avoid overloading the dishwasher as this can prevent the water from circulating and cleaning the dishes.

Use the correct detergent: Always use the correct detergent for your dishwasher. Using the wrong detergent can result in poor cleaning performance, or worse, damage to the dishwasher.

Run the dishwasher when it's full: To save water and energy, it's best to run the dishwasher when it's full. This not only saves resources but also ensures that your dishes are cleaned more efficiently.

Clean the dishwasher regularly: Over time, food debris and mineral buildup can accumulate inside the dishwasher, affecting its performance. To avoid this, make sure to clean the dishwasher regularly by removing any food debris, wiping down the interior, and running a cleaning cycle with a dishwasher cleaner.

Using The Cooker And Microwave

The stove also known as cooker and microwave are two of the most commonly used appliances in the kitchen. They can make cooking and heating up food much easier, but it's important to use them safely and correctly.

The Stove:

Make sure all burners are turned off before you start cooking.

If you're using a gas stove, be sure to light the burner with a long lighter or match.

Use the correct size pot or pan for the burner you are using. A pot that is too small or too large can cause uneven cooking and might even be dangerous.

Turn pot handles away from the front of the stove to prevent accidental spills.

Always keep an eye on what you're cooking, especially if you're using high heat.

The Microwave:

Before using the microwave, make sure there is nothing metal inside. Metal can cause sparks and damage the microwave.

Use microwave-safe containers and cover the food with a microwave-safe lid or plastic wrap.

Don't overheat food in the microwave, as this can cause it to explode or catch fire.
Be careful when removing food from the microwave, as it can be very hot.

Remember, always ask an adult for help if you're not sure how to use an appliance safely. By following these tips, you can use the stove and microwave with confidence and avoid accidents.

Another important thing to remember when operating the stove is to never leave it unattended while in use. This means that you should always stay in the kitchen and keep an eye on what you're cooking. If you need to step away for a moment, turn off the stove or ask someone to watch it for you.

It's also important to make sure that you use the correct cookware on the stove. This means using pots and pans that are the right size for the burners and made from materials that can withstand the heat. For example, you should never use plastic or paper containers on the stove, as they can melt or catch on fire. By following these simple tips, you can help prevent accidents and keep yourself and your home safe while using the stove.

The microwave is a handy appliance that many households have. It's a fast and easy way to heat up leftovers or make popcorn. However, it's important to use it safely and correctly. When using the microwave, make sure you read the instructions carefully and follow them closely.

One important thing to keep in mind is that some materials, like metal or foil, should not be put in the microwave. It's also important to use microwave-safe containers and cover them with a microwave-safe lid or vented plastic wrap. This will help prevent steam from building up and causing a mess or even an explosion.

When using the microwave, it's important to know how to set the time and power level correctly. You should also stir or rotate the food occasionally to help ensure it heats evenly. And always be careful when removing food from the microwave, as it can be very hot and the container might be too hot to handle.

Overall, using the microwave can be a great way to make cooking and reheating food faster and easier. Just be sure to use it safely and correctly.

Employing The Vacuum Cleaner

Keeping a home clean is important for a healthy and happy living environment. One of the most important tools for keeping a home clean is a vacuum cleaner. A vacuum cleaner is a machine that sucks up dirt, dust, and debris from the floors and carpets.

Here are some steps to follow for using a vacuum cleaner:

Prepare the vacuum cleaner by plugging it into an outlet and attaching the hose and accessories.

Adjust the height of the vacuum cleaner according to the type of floor or carpet being cleaned.

Turn on the vacuum cleaner and begin cleaning in one corner of the room. Work your way across the room in a back and forth motion, overlapping each pass.

Use the attachments to clean tight spaces and hard-to-reach areas, such as corners, baseboards, and furniture.

Once you've finished vacuuming, turn off the vacuum cleaner and unplug it from the outlet.

Empty the vacuum cleaner bag or dustbin and clean the filters.

Store the vacuum cleaner in a clean and dry area.

It's important to keep safety in mind when using a vacuum cleaner. Make sure that the area you're vacuuming is clear of any obstacles, such as toys or cords, to avoid tripping. Additionally, always read the instruction manual and follow all safety precautions when using any appliance.

By learning how to use the vacuum cleaner, you'll be able to keep your home clean and tidy. Remember to always clean up any messes as soon as possible to prevent them from accumulating and becoming harder to clean.

Using a vacuum cleaner can be a bit intimidating at first, but with some practice, it can be quite easy. Before starting, make sure that the area you are going to vacuum is clear of any large objects that might get sucked up. Once you have done that, plug in the vacuum cleaner and turn it on.

Next, make sure that the vacuum is set to the correct height for the type of flooring you will be cleaning. If the vacuum is set too high or too low, it won't be as effective at picking up dirt and debris.

Now, you're ready to start vacuuming. Hold the handle and slowly move the vacuum cleaner back and forth in straight lines across the floor. You don't need to push too hard or move too quickly, just let the vacuum do the work.

As you vacuum, keep an eye on the canister or bag to make sure it doesn't get too full. If it does, stop and empty it before continuing.

Finally, when you're finished vacuuming, turn off the machine and unplug it. Take a moment to clean the brush roll and any other attachments that you used, and store the vacuum cleaner in a safe place until the next time you need it.

Remember, it's important to take care of your vacuum cleaner so that it will last a long time. Empty the canister or change the bag regularly, clean the brush roll, and replace any filters as needed. By following these simple steps, you'll be able to keep your home clean and tidy with ease.

How To Cook

Cooking is an important life skill that every child should learn. It is not only fun but also teaches you how to make delicious and healthy meals. In this chapter, you will learn the basics of cooking, such as how to measure ingredients, how to use utensils, and how to follow recipes.

Cooking is a great way to express your creativity, and it allows you to experiment with different flavors and ingredients. But before you can start cooking, you need to learn some basic skills. Here are a few things to keep in mind when you start cooking:

Safety first: Before you start cooking, make sure you know how to handle kitchen tools and equipment safely. Always use oven mitts to protect your hands when handling hot pots and pans. Also, be sure to turn off the stove or oven when you're finished cooking.

Read the recipe: Before you start cooking, read the recipe carefully. Make sure you have all the ingredients you need, and that you understand the cooking process. If you're not sure about something, ask an adult for help.

Measure carefully: Cooking is a science, and accurate measurements are important. Use measuring cups and spoons to make sure you're using the right amount of ingredients.

Prepare ingredients: Before you start cooking, prepare all your ingredients. This means washing, peeling, chopping, and measuring everything before you begin.

Follow instructions: When you're cooking, follow the recipe instructions carefully. Pay attention to cooking times and temperatures, and be sure to stir or mix ingredients when the recipe calls for it.

By following these basic guidelines, you'll be on your way to becoming a great cook. Cooking is a fun and rewarding skill, and with practice, you'll be able to make delicious meals for yourself and your family.

In the next few subchapters, we'll cover some basic cooking skills.

Knowing The Fundamentals

Cooking is an important life skill that everyone should learn. It's fun and can be a great way to express your creativity. One of the first steps in learning to cook is to master the basics. In this subchapter, we'll explore some easy basics that you can learn to prepare by yourself.

<u>Making scrambled eggs:</u>

Scrambled eggs are a breakfast favorite and easy to make. Here's how you can prepare scrambled eggs by yourself:

-Crack two eggs into a bowl
-Add a tablespoon of milk and a pinch of salt and pepper
-Whisk the mixture together until well combined
-Heat a non-stick pan on medium heat
-Add a tablespoon of butter or oil to the pan
-Pour the egg mixture into the pan
-Stir gently with a spatula until the eggs start to set
-When the eggs are cooked to your liking, remove the pan from the heat and transfer the eggs to a plate

Making toast:

Toast is a staple food that can be enjoyed for breakfast, lunch or even as a snack. Here's how you can make toast by yourself:

-Place two slices of bread in a toaster
-Press down the lever or button to start toasting
-Wait for the toast to pop up
-Remove the toast from the toaster and place it on a plate
-Spread butter or your favorite topping on the toast

Boiling pasta

Pasta is an easy and quick meal that you can make by yourself. Here's how to boil pasta:

-Fill a large pot with water and add a pinch of salt
-Place the pot on the stove and turn on the heat to high
-When the water starts boiling, add the pasta

-Stir the pasta occasionally to prevent it from sticking to the pot
-Cook the pasta for the recommended time on the package
-When the pasta is cooked, turn off the heat and drain the water
-Rinse the pasta with cold water to stop the cooking process
-Transfer the pasta to a plate and add your favorite sauce or toppings

By mastering these basic cooking skills, you'll be able to prepare simple meals for yourself and others. Remember to always be careful when using kitchen appliances and to have an adult present when cooking with heat.

Utilizing Kitchen Implements Carefully

In addition to learning how to cook, it is essential to understand how to use kitchen utensils safely. Kitchen utensils are the tools that we use to prepare and cook food. They are essential in cooking, and it is important to handle them with care. Here are some tips on how to use kitchen utensils safely:

Use the right utensils: Different kitchen utensils are designed for specific purposes. For instance, a sharp knife is perfect for slicing while a blunt knife is suitable for spreading. Using the right utensil for the right purpose will help you to avoid accidents and injuries.

Keep your utensils clean and dry: Clean and dry utensils are safe to use. Make sure you wash your utensils after use and dry them before storing them. Clean utensils will not only be safe to use but will also help you maintain hygiene in the kitchen.

Store your utensils properly: Proper storage of your utensils is critical to ensuring their longevity and keeping them safe. Make sure you store your utensils in a dry, clean place where they are easily accessible. Avoid leaving them out in the open as this can lead to accidents.

Handle sharp utensils with care: Sharp knives and other utensils can cause serious injuries if not handled with care. When using sharp utensils, make sure you hold them securely and cut away from your body.

Use oven mitts when handling hot utensils: Hot utensils can cause severe burns if handled without protection. Always use oven mitts or pot holders when handling hot pots and pans.

Use caution when working with electrical appliances: Electrical appliances such as blenders and food processors can cause electrocution if not handled correctly. Make sure you read and follow the manufacturer's instructions before using them.

By following these safety tips, you will be able to handle your kitchen utensils with ease and avoid accidents and injuries.

Remember, safety should always be your top priority when using kitchen utensils.

Preparing Meals Safely With Heat

Cooking can be a fun and rewarding experience, but it can also be dangerous if you don't take the proper safety precautions. Here are some tips on how to cook safely with heat:

Keep an eye on your food: It's important to stay in the kitchen while you're cooking. This way, you can keep an eye on your food and make sure that nothing is burning or boiling over.

Use oven mitts or pot holders: When you're handling hot pots, pans, or dishes, be sure to use oven mitts or pot holders. This will protect your hands from burns and other injuries.

Use the back burners: When you're using the stove, try to use the back burners as much as possible. This will help prevent accidental spills and burns.

Turn pot handles in: Be sure to turn the handles of your pots and pans inwards, towards the center of the stove. This will help prevent accidental spills and burns.

Don't wear loose clothing: When you're cooking, be sure to avoid wearing loose clothing that can catch fire. Instead, wear tight-fitting clothes that are made from fire-resistant materials.

Keep a fire extinguisher nearby: In case of a fire, it's important to have a fire extinguisher nearby. Be sure to read the instructions and know how to use it before you need it.

Never leave the kitchen while cooking: Never leave the kitchen while you're cooking. This can be dangerous and can result in accidental fires or other injuries.

Remember, cooking can be fun and rewarding, but it's important to take the necessary safety precautions to avoid accidents and injuries.

Tidy Up After Cooking

After you've finished cooking, it's important to tidy up the kitchen. Not only will it help keep the kitchen clean and organized, but it will also make cooking easier in the future. Here are some tips for tidying up after cooking:

Wash dishes: Start by washing any dishes that you used while cooking. This will make sure that they're clean and ready to use again the next time you need them.

Put away ingredients: If you used any ingredients that are still out, put them away in their proper place. This will help keep the kitchen organized and make sure that you can find everything you need when you need it.

Clean the counters: Wipe down the counters with a damp cloth to remove any food particles or spills. This will help keep the kitchen clean and hygienic.

Sweep the floor: Use a broom or vacuum to clean up any crumbs or food particles on the floor. This will help prevent any potential safety hazards and make sure that the kitchen is clean.

Take out the trash: If you used any food packaging or scraps, be sure to dispose of them in the trash. This will prevent any potential odors or pests in the kitchen.

By following these steps, you'll have a clean and organized kitchen ready for your next cooking adventure. Remember, cooking is a fun and rewarding activity, but it's important to also take care of the kitchen and keep it tidy.

Attiring Yourself

Learning how to dress yourself is an important skill that every child should learn. Being able to choose your clothes, put them on, and take them off is an essential part of becoming more independent.

Step 1: Choosing Your Clothes

When you choose your clothes, it's important to consider the weather and the occasion. For example, if it's a hot day, you might want to wear shorts and a t-shirt. If you're going to a party, you might want to wear a dress or a suit. Always make sure your clothes are clean and match well.

Step 2: Putting On Your Clothes

To put on your clothes, start with your underwear, then your shirt or dress, then your pants or skirt. Make sure to put your clothes on the right way. For example, your shirt will have a front and a back. Make sure the front is facing the right way. If you need help, don't be afraid to ask an adult for assistance.

Step 3: Tying Your Shoes

Tying your shoes can be a little tricky at first, but with practice, you will get the hang of it. Start by making a loop with one lace, then make a loop with the other lace. Cross the loops over each other, tuck one loop under the other, and pull tight.

Step 4: Taking Off Your Clothes

To take off your clothes, start with your pants or skirt, then your shirt or dress, then your underwear. Take off one item at a time and put them in the laundry basket if they're dirty or hang them up if they're clean.

Step 5: Staying Organized

Make sure to put your clothes away neatly in your drawers or closet. Keep your shoes in a designated spot so you always know where they are. This will help you find what you need quickly and keep your room tidy.

In summary, learning how to dress yourself is an important part of growing up. Remember to choose clothes that are appropriate for the occasion and weather, put them on correctly, tie your shoes, take them off properly, and stay organized. With practice, you will become more independent and confident in dressing yourself.

Adequate Clothes For The Weather

It's essential to dress appropriately for the weather to feel comfortable and stay healthy. Dressing appropriately for the weather can be a challenge, especially if you're new to it. However, with a few tips, you can learn to dress for any weather condition.

First, check the weather forecast. This step is crucial to know what to expect from the weather that day. You can easily find the weather forecast on your smartphone or television. Once you know what the weather will be like, you can decide what clothes to wear.

On hot days, wear light, breathable fabrics, such as cotton or linen, that allow air to circulate and evaporate sweat. It's also essential to wear a hat and sunscreen to protect yourself from the sun's harmful rays.

On cold days, wear layers to trap warm air between them. Start with a base layer of thermal underwear, then add a sweater or fleece jacket, and finish with a windproof and waterproof coat. You'll also want to wear gloves, a hat, and a scarf to protect your extremities from the cold.

During rainy days, wear a waterproof jacket and rain boots to keep your clothes dry. Don't forget an umbrella to protect your head and shoulders from the rain.

In summary, dressing appropriately for the weather requires checking the weather forecast and selecting the right clothes for the occasion. Make sure to wear light and breathable fabrics on hot days, layers on cold days, and waterproof clothes on rainy days. Always consider wearing hats, gloves, and sunscreen, depending on the weather conditions.

In addition to dressing appropriately for the weather, it's important to consider the time of day and the activities you will be doing. For example, if you're going to be outside during the day, you may want to wear a hat to protect your face and sunglasses to protect your eyes. You should also wear sunscreen to protect your skin from the sun's harmful rays.

If you're going to be playing sports or doing any physical activity, it's important to wear comfortable, flexible clothing that allows for a full range of motion. This may include wearing athletic shoes or cleats, depending on the sport.

Another important consideration when dressing for the weather is layering. Layering allows you to adjust your clothing as the temperature changes throughout the day. For example, you might wear a t-shirt and shorts during the warmest part of the day, but then add a sweater or jacket as the temperature cools off in the evening.

By dressing appropriately for the weather and your activities, you'll be able to stay comfortable and safe throughout the day. And don't forget to always wear appropriate shoes for the activity you will be doing.

Recombine Your Wardrobe

As you grow up, you'll have more and more responsibilities and things to do. It's important to learn how to manage your time and prioritize your tasks. Dressing up is one of those tasks that can take up a lot of time if you're not careful. But don't worry, there are ways to make it easier and faster.

One way to do that is to learn how to mix and match your wardrobe. This means that you can create different outfits by using the same clothes but pairing them differently. It's a great way to save time and energy, and it can be a lot of fun too.

Here are some tips to help you mix and match your wardrobe:

Choose clothes that can be worn in different ways. For example, a plain white t-shirt can be worn with jeans, shorts, skirts, or under a sweater or cardigan.

Stick to a color scheme. If you choose clothes that are in the same color family, it's easier to mix and match them. You can also add a pop of color with a scarf, a belt, or a piece of jewelry.

Layer your clothes. You can wear a t-shirt under a button-up shirt or sweater, or add a vest or a scarf to your outfit.

Don't be afraid to experiment. Try different combinations and see what works best for you. If you're not sure, ask a friend or a family member for their opinion.

Keep your clothes clean and in good condition. If you take care of your clothes, they will last longer and look better. Make sure to follow the washing instructions on the label and to iron or steam your clothes if needed.

Mixing and matching your wardrobe can be a lot of fun, and it can also help you express your personality and creativity. Don't be afraid to try new things and to be yourself. With a little bit of practice, you'll become a pro at dressing up in no time.

Attire Yourself For The Occasion

Sometimes, you may need to dress up for a special occasion. Dressing up means wearing clothes that are nicer than your everyday clothes. It's important to know what to wear for different events and occasions.

If you are going to a wedding or a fancy party, you may need to wear a dress or a suit. If you are going to a school dance, you might wear a dress or a nice shirt and pants. If you are going to a sports game, you might wear a jersey or a shirt with your favorite team's logo.

It's important to think about what kind of occasion it is and what kind of clothes would be appropriate. If you are not sure what to wear, you can ask someone for advice. Your parents, siblings, or friends may be able to help you decide what to wear.

Remember, dressing up can be fun, but it's also important to feel comfortable in what you're wearing. Make sure your clothes fit well and that you can move around easily. You don't want to be tugging at your clothes or feeling uncomfortable all night.

It's also important to keep in mind any dress codes or guidelines for the event or occasion. Some events may have a specific dress code, such as "black tie" or "business casual," and it's important to follow these rules.

By dressing appropriately for different occasions, you will feel more confident and be able to enjoy the event or occasion. Plus, it's always fun to dress up and try out different styles and outfits!

Formal Events

There may come a time when you have to dress up for a formal event, such as a wedding or a fancy dinner. It's important to know how to dress appropriately for these occasions.

For boys, a nice suit or dress pants and a dress shirt will do the trick. You can add a tie or a bowtie to complete the look. Black dress shoes are the best choice, but make sure they are polished and clean.

For girls, a pretty dress or a skirt and blouse are perfect choices. High heels are nice, but make sure they're comfortable enough to walk and dance in. Accessorize with simple jewelry and a clutch or small purse.

Remember that you don't have to spend a lot of money to dress nicely. Look for sales and discounts at department stores, or ask your parents if they have any clothes that might fit the occasion.

It's also important to take good care of your formal clothing. Make sure you store it properly, such as on hangers in a closet or a garment bag, and follow the care instructions on the label. You don't want to ruin your nice clothes by accidentally washing them in hot water or putting them in the dryer.

Dressing up for a formal event can be fun and exciting. It's a chance to show off your style and look your best. Just remember to dress appropriately for the occasion, take care of your clothing, and most importantly, have fun!

Clothing For School

Going to school is an important part of every kid's life. It's where you learn new things, make friends, and grow as a person. While it's important to focus on your studies, it's also essential to dress appropriately for school.

The first thing to consider when dressing for school is the dress code. Most schools have a dress code that specifies what you can and cannot wear. Make sure you are familiar with the rules, and always follow them.

When it comes to choosing what to wear, comfort is key. You'll be sitting in class for several hours, so you want to wear clothes that are comfortable and allow you to move around freely. Jeans, leggings, and sweatpants are all great choices. You can pair them with a t-shirt, hoodie, or sweater for a relaxed look.

If you prefer something more formal, you can wear khakis or slacks with a button-down shirt. A dress or skirt is also a good choice for girls, as long as they are of an appropriate length.

Shoes are also important. Sneakers, flats, or loafers are all good choices. Avoid wearing flip-flops or sandals, as they are not safe for running around on the playground.

Accessories can also add a touch of personality to your outfit. A watch, a necklace, or a bracelet can all be great choices. However, keep in mind that too much bling can be distracting and may not be allowed under your school's dress code.

Remember, dressing appropriately for school shows respect for yourself, your teachers, and your classmates. It also helps you focus on your studies without any unnecessary distractions.

Navigation Capability

As you grow up, you will start going places on your own or with your friends and family. It is important to have good navigation skills to be able to go to new places and find your way back home. Here are some tips to help you improve your navigation skills.

Use a Map

A map is a helpful tool to find your way around new places. You can get a map of your city or town from a bookstore or online. Use it to plan your route and mark the important landmarks on your way. Always keep the map with you, so that you can refer to it whenever you need to.

Use GPS

GPS stands for Global Positioning System. It is a tool that helps you find your location and get directions to your destination. You can use a GPS device or a GPS-enabled smartphone app to navigate your way. Be sure to check the route before you start, so you know where you are going.

Learn Directions

Learning directions is important to navigate without relying on maps or GPS. Practice identifying the north, south, east, and west directions in your local area. Once you know the directions, you can use them to orient yourself and navigate your way.

Observe Landmarks

Landmarks are things that stand out in the environment, such as a tall building, a park, or a statue. Observing landmarks can help you find your way around, and remember routes. When you are walking or driving, take note of the landmarks you see on your way.

Plan Your Route

Before you set out, plan your route. This means identifying the best way to get to your destination. Consider the distance, the mode of transportation, the time it will take, and the landmarks you will encounter along the way. This will help you navigate your way more confidently.

Ask for Directions

When all else fails, don't be afraid to ask for directions. You can ask a store owner, a police officer, or a passerby. People are usually willing to help if you approach them politely. If you get lost, don't panic. Take a deep breath, retrace your steps, and try to find your way back on track.

Navigating your way around new places can be an exciting adventure. With these tips, you can improve your navigation skills and find your way around like a pro!

How To Read A Map

Knowing how to read a map is an important navigation skill that can help you find your way around. A map is a drawing that shows you what an area looks like from above. Maps can be used to find directions, locate places, and plan routes.

Here are some steps to follow when reading a map:

Understand the symbols: Maps use symbols to represent things like roads, buildings, and bodies of water. Make sure you know what each symbol represents.

Read the legend: The legend is a key that explains the symbols used on the map. It tells you what each symbol means and what it represents.

Find north: Most maps have a compass rose that shows you which way is north. Knowing which way is north will help you figure out the directions to other places on the map.

Study the scale: Maps are drawn to scale, which means that the distances on the map are proportional to the distances in real life. Check the scale to understand how far apart places are on the map.

Plan your route: Once you have figured out where you are and where you want to go, you can plan your route by following the roads and landmarks on the map.

Keep the map oriented: As you move around, make sure to keep the map oriented so that north is always at the top. This will help you keep your bearings and stay on track.

By following these steps, you can learn how to read a map and use it to navigate. Remember that practice makes perfect, so don't be afraid to practice reading maps until you become an expert!

How To Read A Compass

Compasses are tools that can help you navigate and find your way around. They are useful in many situations, like when you are hiking or camping, or even when you are driving in a new place. A compass can tell you which direction you are facing and can help you figure out how to get where you need to go.

Here are some tips on how to read a compass:

Understand the Parts of a Compass: A compass has a needle that points towards magnetic north, which is different from true north. The needle sits on a rotating card that is marked with degrees. The outer edge of the compass is also marked with degrees.

Set Your Compass: Hold your compass flat and turn it until the needle lines up with the orienting arrow. Make sure the north end of the needle points to the "N" on the compass.

Determine Your Heading: Look at the degree markings on the compass to determine the direction you need to travel. For example, if you need to go east, turn your body until the "E" on the compass is in line with the direction you want to go.

Follow Your Bearing: Once you have your heading, keep your compass level and in front of you as you walk. Make sure the needle stays pointing to the "N" on the compass. Use landmarks, such as trees or rocks, to help you stay on course.
Adjust for Declination: In some areas, magnetic north and true north are different. This is called declination. You can adjust for declination by using a map or looking up the declination in your area and adjusting the direction you are traveling accordingly.

Remember to always use a compass in conjunction with a map and to practice your skills before heading out into the wilderness. With practice, you'll become a pro at using a compass and navigating your way around.

Requesting The Way

Even with a map or compass, there may be times when you need to ask for directions. It's important to know how to do this in a polite and respectful way. Here are some tips to keep in mind:

Look for someone who appears approachable and friendly. They should be someone who you feel comfortable talking to.

Begin by greeting the person and introducing yourself. Say something like "Hello, my name is Emily. Can you please help me find my way to the library?"

Be clear about where you need to go. Use specific names of streets or landmarks if possible. This will help the person give you more accurate directions.
Listen carefully to the person's response. If you're not sure you understand what they're saying, ask them to repeat it.

Thank the person for their help, even if their directions weren't exactly what you were looking for. It's always good to be polite and show gratitude.

Remember, asking for directions is a normal part of life, and there's no need to feel embarrassed or ashamed if you need to do it. Everyone gets lost sometimes, and it's better to ask for help than to keep wandering around aimlessly.

Quest And Research Capability

As a child, it's important to learn how to study and do research. In school, you will have to study for tests and complete research projects, so it's good to learn these skills early on. Here are some tips to help you study and do research like a pro.

Create a Study Schedule: To study effectively, you need to have a plan. Create a study schedule that outlines when you will study and for how long. Stick to your schedule and make it a habit. This will help you stay organized and on track.

Find a quiet Place to Study: Find a quiet place to study where you can focus and avoid distractions. Turn off your phone or put it on silent, and let your family members know that you need some quiet time.

Take Notes: Taking notes is an important part of studying. It helps you remember important information and also helps you stay focused during class. You can use a notebook or digital device to take notes.

Use Flashcards: Flashcards are a great tool for studying. You can create flashcards with questions on one side and answers on the other. You can then use these flashcards to test yourself and practice memorization.

Use Online Resources: There are many online resources available to help you study and research. Websites like Khan Academy, Quizlet, and Scholastic can be great resources for learning and practicing new material.

Use a Dictionary and Thesaurus: When you come across a word you don't know, it's important to look it up. Using a dictionary and thesaurus can help you expand your vocabulary and better understand the material you are studying.

Take Breaks: It's important to take breaks while studying to avoid burnout. Take a short break every 30 minutes or so to stretch, walk around, or grab a healthy snack.

Use Critical Thinking: When researching a topic, it's important to use critical thinking. This means looking at multiple sources and evaluating the information to determine what is accurate and trustworthy.

Keep Track of Sources: When doing research, it's important to keep track of your sources. Write down the title of the article or book, the author, and the publication date. This will help you cite your sources properly and avoid plagiarism.

Organize Your Research: After you've completed your research, organize your notes and materials. Create an outline to help you structure your research paper or presentation.

Ask for help: If you are struggling with a particular subject or concept, don't be afraid to ask for help. This could mean talking to your teacher, a tutor, or a friend who is knowledgeable in the subject. Asking for help can save you time and frustration in the long run.

By following these tips, you can become a successful student and researcher. Remember, the more you practice, the better you will become. Good luck!

Learning In Bits And Pieces

Learning is a never-ending process. We are always learning, even when we don't realize it. However, sometimes we need to be more intentional in our learning, especially when we're studying for school or trying to gain new knowledge or skills. Learning in bits and pieces is one way to achieve this.

When we say "learning in bits and pieces," we mean breaking down a larger topic or subject into smaller, more manageable pieces. This can help make it easier to understand and remember information. For example, if you're trying to learn about the solar system, it can be overwhelming to try and learn everything at once. Instead, try breaking it down into smaller parts, like learning about each planet one at a time.

Here are some tips for learning in bits and pieces:

Set small goals: Instead of trying to learn everything at once, set small goals for yourself. For example, if you're studying for a test, aim to learn one section at a time.

Take breaks: It's important to take breaks when studying, especially when learning in bits and pieces. Take short breaks every 20-30 minutes to give your brain a chance to rest and recharge.

Use visual aids: Visual aids like diagrams, charts, and pictures can be helpful when learning in bits and pieces. They can help break down complex information into smaller, more manageable pieces.

Review and reinforce: It's important to review what you've learned and reinforce the information in your mind. One way to do this is to create flashcards or quizzes to test your knowledge.

Learning in bits and pieces can be a great way to make studying and learning more manageable and less overwhelming. Give it a try and see how it can help you with your learning and studying!

Here are some more tips for learning in bits and pieces:

Take advantage of small bits of free time. If you have a few minutes to spare, use that time to review vocabulary words, read a few pages of a book, or practice math problems. These small bits of time can add up over the course of a day or week.

Set specific goals for what you want to accomplish during your study sessions. This will help you stay focused and motivated, and will make it easier to break your studies into manageable chunks.

Use mnemonic devices to help you remember important information. Mnemonic devices are tricks or tools that help you remember things. For example, you might use a phrase like "My very eager mother just served us nine pizzas" to remember the order of the planets in our solar system (Mercury, Venus, Earth, Mars, Jupiter, Saturn, Uranus, Neptune, and Pluto).

Take frequent breaks to avoid burnout. It can be tempting to study for long periods of time without taking breaks, but this can actually be counterproductive. Taking breaks helps your brain process information and stay fresh.

Use repetition to help you remember important information. The more times you see or hear something, the more likely you are to remember it. Consider making flashcards or writing out important information by hand to help reinforce it in your memory.

Making Notes

Taking notes is a skill that can help you remember important information from classes, meetings, and books. There are many ways to take notes, and you should find the method that works best for you. Here are some tips for taking effective notes:

Listen actively: To take good notes, you need to be an active listener. This means paying attention to what the speaker is saying, focusing on the main points, and ignoring distractions.

Use abbreviations: When taking notes, you don't have to write out every word. Instead, use abbreviations to save time and space. For example, you can use "w/" for "with," "b/c" for "because," and "e.g." for "for example."

Use bullet points: Instead of writing in full sentences, use bullet points to organize your notes. This makes it easier to see the main ideas and relationships between them.

Highlight key points: You can use highlighters or underline important words or phrases to make them stand out. This will help you remember them later when you review your notes.

Use diagrams and drawings: Sometimes, a picture is worth a thousand words. Use diagrams and drawings to illustrate concepts or processes. This can help you remember information better and make connections between ideas.

Review your notes: It's important to review your notes regularly. This will help you retain the information and identify areas where you need more clarification or explanation.

Remember, taking good notes is a skill that can be developed over time. With practice and experimentation, you can find the method that works best for you and make the most of your note-taking abilities.

Create Your Own Research Room

Creating a designated study space is important to help you focus and concentrate on your studies. Your study space should be a place where you feel comfortable and productive. Here are some tips to help you create a study space that works for you:

Choose a quiet area: Find a spot in your home that is quiet and away from distractions like the TV or video games.

Set up a desk or table: You should have a flat surface to work on, like a desk or table. Make sure it is the right height for you and has enough space for your study materials.

Use good lighting: Make sure your study space is well-lit. Use natural light if possible, and add a lamp if needed.

Keep it organized: Keep your study space clean and organized. Use folders, binders, and shelves to store your study materials.

Add some decorations: Make your study space a place you enjoy being in by adding some decorations. Hang up some motivational posters or pictures of things you like.

Make it comfortable: You should feel comfortable in your study space. Use a comfortable chair and add a cushion or pillow for back support.

Keep it distraction-free: Remove any distractions from your study space, like your phone or video games. This will help you focus on your studies.

Remember, your study space should be a place that helps you concentrate and get your work done. Don't be afraid to experiment with different set-ups until you find what works best for you.

Unthinking

Unthinking is a great way to get your brain to relax and to take a break. It means doing something that doesn't require a lot of thinking, like taking a walk or listening to music.

When you are studying or researching, it's important to take breaks to give your brain a rest. You can't just keep going and going without giving your brain a break.

If you find yourself feeling tired or getting frustrated, it's a good time to unthink. Doing something that doesn't require a lot of thinking can help your brain recharge and get ready for more learning.

Unthinking can also help you be more creative. When you're not actively trying to think of something, your brain can come up with new ideas and solutions.

So, take a break and do something you enjoy. It could be playing a game, drawing, or even just taking a nap. Unthinking can help you learn better and be more productive in the long run.

Unthinking is, in its second meaning, an important skill that can help you learn more efficiently. It involves paying attention to what you're doing and actively engaging with the material you're studying. When you unthink, you let go of any distractions and focus solely on your work.

To unthink, you can start by finding a quiet, comfortable place to study. Remove any distractions such as electronic devices and turn off the television. You can also try deep breathing or meditation to help clear your mind.

It's also helpful to break your work into smaller tasks and take frequent breaks to avoid burnout. When you unthink, you give yourself permission to take a step back and recharge before diving back into your studies.

Remember, unthinking takes practice, so don't get discouraged if you find it difficult at first. With time and persistence, you can improve your ability to focus and retain information.

Here are some more tips to help kids unthink and clear their minds:

Take a break: It's important to take regular breaks to recharge your brain. After 30-45 minutes of focused work, take a quick 10-15 minute break to do something you enjoy. It could be as simple as taking a walk, playing with your pet, or listening to your favorite music.

Practice mindfulness: Mindfulness is a technique that involves focusing your attention on the present moment. It can help you clear your mind and reduce stress. There are many mindfulness activities you can try, such as deep breathing, meditation, or yoga.

Get enough sleep: Getting enough sleep is essential for a healthy mind and body. It helps your brain recharge and consolidate your learning. Most kids need between 9-11 hours of sleep every night, so make sure you are getting enough rest.

Stay organized: Staying organized can help reduce stress and make studying more efficient. Use a planner or calendar to keep track of important dates, make to-do lists, and keep your study materials in order.

Stay active: Regular physical activity can help improve focus and concentration. It's also a great way to reduce stress and improve your overall health. Find an activity you enjoy, such as playing a sport, dancing, or going for a bike ride, and try to make it a regular part of your routine.

Self-Amusement

As you grow up, you'll find that it's important to have hobbies and activities that you enjoy doing in your free time. Whether you're feeling bored, stressed, or just need a break, having a list of fun and engaging things to do can make all the difference. Here are some ideas for self-entertainment:

Read a book: Reading is a great way to escape into new worlds and learn new things. Choose books that interest you and challenge you to think in new ways.

Play games: There are many games you can play by yourself, like puzzles, crosswords, and Sudoku. Or you can play video games or board games with friends and family.

Listen to music: Music can help you relax or energize, depending on the type of music you choose. Create playlists of your favorite songs or discover new artists.

Try arts and crafts: Drawing, painting, knitting, or sewing are all great ways to express your creativity and make something unique.

Learn something new: Take online courses or tutorials to learn new skills like cooking, coding, or a new language.

Exercise: Physical activity is good for your body and mind. Try yoga, running, dancing, or any other activity you enjoy.

Watch movies and TV shows: There are so many great movies and TV shows to watch, whether you want to laugh, cry, or learn something new.

Go outside: Spend time in nature, go for a walk, or try a new outdoor activity like camping or kayaking.

Remember, self-entertainment doesn't have to be expensive or complicated. You can find joy and relaxation in simple activities like taking a warm bath or enjoying a cup of tea. Whatever you choose, make sure it's something you enjoy and that brings you happiness.

Applying Technology For Your Needs

Technology has become an integral part of our lives, and it can be a great tool for learning, playing and entertaining. Here are some tips on how to use technology to keep yourself entertained.

Learning: Technology has made learning more accessible and interactive than ever before. You can use the internet to research any topic that interests you. There are also many educational apps and websites that you can use to learn new skills or practice what you already know. Some of the most popular educational websites are Khan Academy, Coursera and edX.

<u>Playing:</u> There are many ways to play games using technology. You can play games on your phone, tablet, or computer. There are many free games available on app stores and websites, or you can purchase games for more advanced gameplay. Some popular games include Fortnite, Minecraft, and Roblox.

<u>Entertaining:</u> Technology can be used to watch movies, TV shows, and listen to music. Streaming services like Netflix, Hulu, and Spotify provide unlimited access to a vast library of movies, TV shows, and music. You can also use YouTube to watch videos on any topic that interests you.

<u>Staying Safe:</u> While technology is a great tool for entertainment, it's essential to stay safe online. Be careful about the information you share online, and never give out personal information to strangers. Make sure your privacy settings are set up correctly, and always use strong passwords.

Remember, technology is an excellent tool for learning, playing, and entertainment, but it's also essential to take breaks and engage in other activities. So, make sure to balance your time spent on technology with other activities like exercise, reading, and spending time with friends and family.

Participating In STEM Contests

STEM (Science, Technology, Engineering, and Mathematics) challenges are a fun way to learn while also being entertained. STEM stands for Science, Technology, Engineering, and

Mathematics. By combining these subjects, we can come up with exciting challenges that you can create and solve on your own. Here are some tips for creating your own STEM challenges:

Choose a theme: The first step is to decide what your STEM challenge will be about. You could choose a theme like space exploration, building bridges, or designing robots.

Gather materials: Once you've chosen your theme, it's time to gather the materials you'll need. Look around your home or school for materials you can use. You might need things like cardboard boxes, paper, tape, scissors, or building blocks.

Plan your challenge: Now that you have your theme and materials, it's time to plan your challenge. Think about what you want to achieve and how you'll measure success. For example, if you're designing a robot, you might want to see how far it can move, how fast it can go, or how well it can turn.

Build and test: With your plan in place, it's time to start building. Follow your plan and use the materials you gathered to create your challenge. Once you're done building, it's time to test your creation. Try out your challenge and see how well it works. If it doesn't work the first time, don't worry. Try making adjustments and try again.

Reflect and improve: After you've tested your STEM challenge, it's time to reflect on how it went. Think about what worked well and what could be improved. Use this knowledge to improve your challenge and try again.

Creating STEM challenges is a great way to learn and have fun at the same time. With a little creativity and some basic materials, you can create your own challenges that are both challenging and entertaining. So why not give it a try and see what you can create?

A great example of a STEM challenge is to build a bridge using only paper and tape that can hold the weight of a toy car. This challenge incorporates the principles of engineering and physics, and it can be a fun and engaging way to learn about these subjects.

Here's how you could plan and execute this challenge:

Gather your materials: You will need paper and tape, as well as a toy car to test the bridge's weight capacity.
Research and learn: Before starting the challenge, it's a good idea to learn about bridges and the principles of engineering and physics that are involved in their design and construction. You can use books, online resources, or videos to research these topics.

Plan your design: Now it's time to start designing your bridge. Think about the different shapes and designs that might work, and draw out your plan on paper. Consider things like the length of the bridge, the height, and the angles of the supports.

Build your bridge: Using the materials you've gathered, it's time to start building your bridge. Be sure to follow your design carefully, and make adjustments as necessary.

Test your bridge: Once your bridge is complete, it's time to test it with the toy car. Place the car on the bridge and see if it holds up under the weight. If it doesn't, think about what you can change to make it stronger.

Reflect and iterate: After you've tested your bridge, take some time to reflect on the process. What worked well? What could have been improved? Use what you've learned to make adjustments to your design and try the challenge again.

STEM challenges like this one can be a great way to learn about science, technology, engineering, and math in a fun and engaging way. By planning and executing your own challenge, you can develop important skills like problem-solving, critical thinking, and creativity.

How To Deal With Bullies

Unfortunately, bullies exist, and they can make life unpleasant for their targets. However, there are ways to deal with them. Here are some tips for dealing with bullies:

Stay calm and confident Bullies often target those who appear weak or unsure of themselves. By staying calm and confident, you can avoid becoming a target. Stand tall, make eye contact, and speak in a clear, assertive voice.

Ignore the bully Sometimes, bullies are seeking attention, and ignoring them can take away their power. This may involve walking away or focusing on something else. Bullies may lose interest if they feel they are not getting a reaction.

Seek help If you are being bullied, seek help from a trusted adult or friend. This could be a teacher, parent, coach, or guidance counselor. They can provide support and help you come up with a plan to deal with the bully.

Use humor Sometimes, using humor can defuse a situation with a bully. However, it is important to use humor in a way that does not come across as mean-spirited or defensive. Try to make light of the situation without belittling the bully.

Stand up for yourself It is important to stand up for yourself, but this does not mean physically fighting back. Instead, calmly assert your boundaries and let the bully know that their behavior is not acceptable. For example, you could say, "I don't appreciate being talked to that way, and I would appreciate it if you could speak to me more respectfully."

Don't blame yourself Remember that bullying is not your fault. You have the right to be treated with respect and kindness, and no one deserves to be bullied.

Be a good friend If you see someone being bullied, stand up for them. Offer support and let them know they are not alone. Sometimes, simply having a friend can make all the difference.

Dealing with bullies can be challenging, but remember that you are not alone. Seek help, stay calm and confident, and stand up for yourself.

What You Can To When Things Go Wild

When you're being bullied, things can quickly get out of hand, and it can be challenging to know what to do. However, there are some things you can do to handle the situation. Here are a few things you can try:

Stay calm: When someone is bullying you, it's easy to get angry or upset, but it's essential to stay calm. If you get upset, it could make the situation worse.

Walk away: Sometimes, the best thing to do is to walk away from the situation. Don't engage with the bully and try to avoid them as much as possible.

Tell an adult: If you're being bullied at school, tell a teacher or another adult you trust. They can help you to deal with the situation and keep you safe.

Stand up for yourself: If you feel comfortable doing so, you can stand up for yourself and tell the bully that their behavior is not okay. However, it's important to do this in a calm and confident manner, and not to escalate the situation.

Practice assertiveness: Sometimes, bullies target people they see as weak or vulnerable. Practicing assertiveness can help you to feel more confident and less vulnerable. You can start by setting boundaries and being clear about what is and isn't acceptable behavior.

Don't blame yourself: Remember that being bullied is not your fault. Don't blame yourself for the bully's behavior or think that you deserve it.

By staying calm, walking away, telling an adult, standing up for yourself, practicing assertiveness, and not blaming yourself, you can handle bullying in a way that keeps you safe and makes you feel empowered.

When things get out of hand and someone starts to bully you or someone you know, there are a few things you can do to handle the situation. The first thing you should do is to stay calm and don't let your emotions get the best of you. It can be tough, but responding with anger or fear can make the situation worse.

Instead, take a deep breath and try to remain composed. Stand up tall and make eye contact with the bully. Bullies are often looking for an easy target, so by showing that you're confident and in control, you're less likely to be a victim.

Next, try to talk to the bully and see if you can resolve the situation peacefully. Sometimes bullies are just looking for attention or a reaction, and if you show that you're not bothered by their behavior, they may lose interest and leave you alone.

If the bully continues to harass you, it's important to seek help from a trusted adult. This could be a teacher, parent, coach, or another responsible adult who can provide support and help you find a solution. Remember, it's not your fault that you're being bullied, and there's no shame in asking for help.

If you witness someone else being bullied, it's important to speak up and offer your support. Let the victim know that you're there for them and that they're not alone. You can also report the bullying to a teacher or another adult who can help address the situation.

In some cases, it may be necessary to involve the police or other authorities if the bullying becomes physical or threatening. It's important to remember that everyone has the right to feel safe and respected, and bullying is never acceptable.

Who To Seek Help From When Being Bullied

If you're being bullied, it's important to know who you can turn to for help. There are many people who are there to support you and make sure you are safe.

First, you can always talk to your parents or guardians. They love you and want you to be happy and safe, and they can help you figure out the best way to handle the situation. You can also talk to a teacher or guidance counselor at your school. They are trained to handle situations like this and can help you come up with a plan to deal with the bullying.

If you feel uncomfortable talking to someone in person, you can call or text a helpline. There are many helplines that are available 24/7 and are completely confidential. They can offer support and advice, and help you figure out what steps to take next.

Another option is to talk to a trusted friend or family member. Sometimes, just talking to someone and getting their perspective can help you feel better and give you the strength to stand up to the bully.

Remember, you are not alone, and there are people who want to help you. Don't be afraid to reach out and ask for help.

If you are being bullied, it is important to seek help from a trusted adult. This could be a parent, teacher, coach, or another adult you trust. Sometimes it can be hard to speak up about being bullied, but it is important to remember that you are not alone.

There are also hotlines and organizations you can reach out to for help. The National Bullying Prevention Center, for example, has resources available for kids and parents to help prevent and address bullying. The StopBullying.gov website also offers tips and resources for kids who are dealing with bullying.

It's important to remember that you have the right to feel safe and respected, and no one has the right to make you feel otherwise. Speaking up and seeking help is a brave and important step in putting an end to bullying.

How To React When A Known Person Is Being Bullied

It can be challenging to know what to do when someone you know is being bullied. But there are some things you can do to help them out.

Firstly, it's important to let the person know that you care about them and that you are there for them. Sometimes, just listening to their concerns and feelings can help. Be supportive and let them know that they are not alone.

If you witness the bullying, you can step in and intervene. It's essential to do so in a calm and collected manner. You can try to diffuse the situation by speaking up and distracting the bully or by getting other people involved. Remember to be safe and never put yourself in harm's way.

If you are not comfortable confronting the bully, or you feel it may make the situation worse, you can report the bullying to a trusted adult. This could be a teacher, counselor, parent, or other authority figure. They can help take action to stop the bullying and keep the person safe.

It's important to keep in mind that bullying is never the victim's fault, and it's not okay. So, it's crucial to speak up and take action when you see or hear about bullying. Together, we can help put an end to it.

When you see someone being bullied, it is essential to act, and there are several ways to do that. If you are in a group, you can stand up for the person being bullied by speaking out against the bully's actions or by stepping in to stop the bullying. You can offer support to the person being bullied by talking to them and letting them know that they are not alone. Sometimes all it takes is one person to show that they care to make a difference.

Another way to help someone being bullied is to report the bullying to a trusted adult. If you are in school, this could be a teacher, school counselor, or principal. If you are outside of school, you can report the bullying to a parent or other adult. Reporting the bullying can help to stop it and also shows the person being bullied that someone is looking out for them.

It is also essential to avoid bullying behavior yourself. If you see someone being bullied and do nothing, you are passively condoning the bullying behavior. By treating others with kindness and respect, you can create a culture where bullying is not tolerated.

Remember that bullying is never okay, and there are always ways to help. If you or someone you know is being bullied, speak out and seek help. Together, we can work to create a world where everyone is treated with kindness and respect.

It's important to remember that bullying is not just physical. It can also be emotional or verbal. If you see someone being teased, excluded, or gossiped about, it's important to speak up and offer your support. Sometimes, a simple gesture like inviting the person to join your group or standing up for them can make a big difference.

It's important to never participate in bullying behavior, even if you feel pressure to do so. It's also important to recognize that some people may not feel comfortable standing up to bullies on their own, so it's important to offer your support and report any bullying behavior to a trusted adult.

If you witness bullying, it's important to report it to a teacher, guidance counselor, or other trusted adult as soon as possible. They can help address the situation and make sure that the bullying stops. It's important to be specific about what you've seen or heard and provide as much information as possible to help the adult address the situation.

Remember, bullying can have serious long-term effects on the victim's mental and emotional health. By speaking up and seeking help, you can help stop bullying and create a safer and more positive environment for everyone.

If you witness someone being bullied, it's essential to act in a responsible and safe manner. Here are some tips to help you respond when someone else is being bullied:

Speak up: You can start by telling the bully that their behavior is unacceptable. You can also tell them to stop the behavior or ask them to leave the person alone. Speak up in a calm and assertive manner.

Be a friend: If you see someone being bullied, you can be their friend. You can offer them a shoulder to lean on and be there to listen to them. Let them know that you care and that they are not alone.

Report the incident: You can report the incident to a trusted adult, such as a teacher, counselor, or parent. They can help you take appropriate action to stop the bullying.

Don't join in: You should never participate in bullying, even if you think it's just for fun. It's important to treat others with kindness and respect.

Stand up for what's right: If you see someone being bullied, it's important to stand up for what's right. Let the person being bullied know that you're there for them, and that you won't tolerate bullying. Together, you can make a difference.

Remember, it's always important to be safe when responding to bullying. If you feel that you or someone else is in danger, seek help immediately from a trusted adult or authority figure.

Résumé

Congratulations! You have made it to the end of this book! Over the last several chapters, we have talked about various life skills that can help you navigate the world around you. From communication to self-care to problem-solving, these skills are important for your growth and success.

As you look back on what you have learned, remember that mastering these skills takes practice and patience. You may not get everything right the first time, but that's okay. Keep trying, and with time and effort, you will improve.

In this book, we have covered many topics, but there is always more to learn. As you continue your journey, keep an open mind and be willing to learn from those around you. Take advantage of new opportunities and experiences to keep expanding your knowledge and skills.

Remember, the skills you have learned in this book will be useful in all aspects of your life, from school to work to personal relationships. By being mindful of how you communicate, manage your time, and take care of yourself, you can set yourself up for success and happiness.

As you look ahead, I encourage you to keep striving for growth and learning. The world is constantly changing, and you can be a part of that change. Use your skills and talents to make a positive impact on your community and the world.

Thank you for reading this book, and I wish you all the best on your journey ahead!